CRUX MATTERS

BY J. M. GHEEN

ISBN-13: 978-1484108208
ISBN-10: 1484108205

Author may be professionally contacted via email at JMGheen@gmail.com. Please do not contact Author with solicitations or automated messages.

Cover art by Dave Fymbo:
http://designingebookcovers.blogspot.com

TABLE OF CONTENTS

INTRODUCTION

You are not about to read a document full of thick, boring language. Rather, we are going to explore answers to meaningful questions. You will likely find that these questions and answers have been important to you all along. It is quite possible that some of what we cover will make you uncomfortable. If it helps, keep in mind that I would not have been able to effectively write it down if I had not first learned it personally. In other words, we are in this together.

You have taken the time to read this far, which indicates that you are hoping to find something of value. Keep reading! In the coming pages, we will assemble a framework you can use to address life's biggest questions, including:

- Who is God and what does He have to do with you and me?
- Why does the world look and act the way it does?
- What are we supposed to be doing with our lives?

You might be wondering how on earth a little book like this will be able to provide thoughtful answers to those questions and others. The reason is that this little book is based very carefully on a much bigger book – the Bible. However, we are not going to look at a bunch of Bible verses and try to come up with nice ways of applying those verses to our lives. All too often, the Bible is reduced to verse snippets that are thrown at us as though we are supposed to change everything about our lives because a very old, very thick book said certain words in a certain order. Call me skeptical, but I do not expect a thinking person to bend his or her worldview only because I can present a relevant quote followed by a verse reference. If it were that easy, we could just as well be seeing major religions based on Shakespeare. Whether you have read the Bible extensively or never bothered to pick it up at all, you will probably agree that verse snippets seem to raise more questions than answers, especially when they are thrown about without context or agreement.

So here is what I propose: let's look at the Bible as a whole. I do not mean we are going to take an academic look at Biblical history or tattered remnants of manuscript. There are plenty of books on those subjects - some better than others. What I mean is we are going to look at the whole message of the Bible. We are going to examine the assumptions the Bible presents and test those assumptions to see if they hold together. If God has indeed inspired the Bible, and if He has intended to communicate with us through it, then there is great value to be had in not only reading the words on the page but also in learning to adopt the perspective from which those words were inspired.

Whether you are a long-time student of the Bible or you are merely curious to see what all of the fuss is about, it is well worth making the effort to understand the "big picture" from God's perspective as communicated in the Bible. For the devout Christian, the following pages will give you much to consider in your daily devotions. For the wisdom-seeker, this book details a worldview so potent that it has not only had a drastic shift on the course of human history, but also a profoundly personal impact on how millions of individuals relate to the God of the universe.

The following pages contain very few direct quotes from the Bible. However, throughout the text, I have provided annotations which map to an appendix of relevant and meaningful Bible references. For e-readers, the verses and the appendix are hyperlinked in order that most e-readers can jump to the verse and then return easily to the main text. If you are physically holding a paper copy of this book, just keep a finger in the appendix so you can easily flip to the reference verses and back to the main text. These verses are provided to enable a deeper layer of reading and so that readers who want to make further study of the topics addressed will have handy places to start.

If, by writing this book, I have in any way distorted the truth, I humbly ask your forgiveness and God's forgiveness. No arrangement of words can, in and of itself, give purpose to our lives. It is up to God to work in the hearts for which He has paid so steep a price and it is up to the heart to yield to God's work. It is from one such grateful heart that I write all you find here.

WHO IS GOD?

"Who is God" is a big question. It is too big to answer in a single lifetime, not to mention in a single book. Even so, we ask the question for a good reason. Our concern with God's nature begins with a simple premise: if there is a supreme originating authority in the universe, then you and I must be somehow subject to that authority's desires and designs. In other words, we are here because God, whatever that title entails, wants us to be here. The more we know God, the more we understand our purpose.

A true God, by definition, can shape reality by exercising His will. It is God's prerogative to decide what is, what is not, and what may be or will be. A true God of infinite power and infinite existence must be the absolute origin of all things.[1] Because God is the origin of everything, we humans exist because He made us, either directly or indirectly. Naturally, if He made us then we want to know more about Him. Some say He made us in a few days and some say He did it over billions of years. What matters here is that we humans exist and continue existing because God decided that we ought to.

Why would God create humans? It can only be that He created us because He wanted to. Why does an artist paint pictures? Because painting is meaningful to her. Why do musicians play music? Because their music is an expression of something that matters to them. Why does a retired executive take up woodworking? Because he takes pleasure in working with his hands. Why do we pursue being professionally skilled in our careers? Why does somebody practice her golf swing or his fly fishing technique? Because recreation, progress, mastery, and creative beauty are satisfying and meaningful pursuits. Why did God decide to craft a race of humankind? Like the artist, the hobbyist, the musician, the professional, and the recreator, His craft in its original form is an expression of Himself. God would not create something in His own image but with no use or significance. The God of the universe takes delight in creating something meaningful. He built some of His own qualities into us, His creation, just as we ourselves are inevitably reflected in our own creations. There is a difference, though, between God's creations and your or my creations. Our creations do not tend to have wills of their own. Our creations tend to remain how we created them. We are not God. We cannot author life, nor can we assign life or free will to what we make. The God of the Universe, however, has the ability to breathe life into His creations. You and I are masterpieces of His creativity.[2]

What else do we need to know about God? In addition to being our creator, God is powerful. His power may be the most universally recognized aspect of His being. We use words like "omnipotent" to describe His power. "Omni" is a word that combines to mean "everything" or "all". "Potent" means "power" or "influence". God is "omnipotent" or all-powerful. He answers to nobody but Himself.[3]

God is knowledge. He is omniscient, or all-knowing.[4] There is nothing that can be known, past present or future, which He does not already know.[5] This infinite knowledge is possible partly because He is omnipresent or "everywhere at the same time". There is no force, thought, event, concept, object, or intention of which He is not aware.

God is not conflicted in His decisions because He does not make mistakes.[6] He is all-powerful and all-knowing: He knows all possible courses of action and He knows all possible outcomes of every possible decision. Think carefully about that concept! God knows all actions. Furthermore, He can perfectly predict, or foreknow, every outcome of every action as well as every resulting repercussion of every outcome. Therefore, God could not possibly make any decision that is less than perfect. Nothing is able to surprise God. His judgment is always perfect. When He sets something in motion, He knows exactly if, when, where and how it will come to rest. When He creates a life, He knows exactly how that life will interact with all other lives in existence or intended existence. The old saying that "God doesn't make mistakes" is correct even on the most logical level. Not only does He not make mistakes, He cannot make mistakes. He cannot be forced to do anything against His will. Because He has perfect knowledge and total power, His intent will ultimately manifest. By nature, He will eventually overrule any conflicting intent.[7, 8]

Besides being our creator, God also defines concepts much larger than us. For example, "right" is defined by Him[9] and "wrong" is defined by whatever is not of His nature.[10] Since He cannot make mistakes, whatever He does is "right" in every possible sense. Whatever violates His will is "wrong". Whatever is like Him is "righteous" or "good"[11] and whatever is not like Him is, of course, "not good": the spectrum of not good includes "merely worthless" and extends all the way through "bad" and "evil"[12]. In our small corner of the universe, we humans sometimes come up with our own versions of right and wrong, good and evil. Our ideas of synthesized morality can seem nice on the surface. However, if it is given undeserved precedence, human-made morality attempts to replace God's perfect will with imperfect human judgment. We may find our own versions of right and wrong convenient for a time, but whatever conflicts with God's definition of right must eventually be overruled. It is not in God's nature to ultimately bow His perfect will to a conflicting imperfect will. It is utterly impossible for our will to be more perfect than His will.[13] It makes sense that it would be wrong for Him to replace perfection with imperfection.

Although you and I are capable of some knowledge, some power, and some reasoning,[14] we would be foolish to expect God to violate His own standards in order to accept ours. Why would He? If we disagree with God, we disagree from a position of infinitely less knowledge, perspective, experience, and judgment. Let's face it: we humans are conflicted, confused, mistaken, and guilty on most every issue of morality. We hardly respect each other's opinions on morality even when we try. Our legal systems are often mocked because we cannot consistently sort "right" and "wrong" out between each other. We consistently fail to enforce satisfactory justice. Indeed, we cannot even sort these issues out inside of ourselves. When we know what is right, we frequently do not do it, as is evidenced on local news channels every evening.

The God of the universe, on the other hand has all the knowledge and all the power. We have only whatever He has given us or allowed us to have for a time. No matter how justified we might feel, God's justifications will always be better. He is not a bully that way. It is simply a logical result of the fact that He is God and we are not. By infinite measure, He is better informed, more experienced, more qualified, and has a perfect track record across the board. I would not debate a rocket scientist on rocket booster configurations because I am not a respected authority in physics. Neither would I argue with a Hollywood star about feeling the pressure of the paparazzi because I do not know how it feels to live 24/7 in the public spotlight. It would be foolish of me to argue with those who actually define their very disciplines or who have a more informed perspective than I have. In the same way and even more so, we would be foolish to expect God, the author and justifier of all morality, to accept our opinions on morality over His own, absolute morality.

Besides being the Creator and the Definer, God is infinite. "Finite" is to be measured, to be bounded, subject to space, time, circumstances, or the wills of others. God is the measurer, the One who draws boundaries. His will is the Will to which all others are ultimately subjected. How interesting that God defines, making things DEfinite while He Himself is

INfinite. He defines all else with respect to Himself[15] but He cannot be defined except that, well, He is God. He is Himself (in infinite terms, "he" does not confine to a stereotypical human gender). God pales in comparison to nothing while all time, space, measurements, objects, powers, and beings, pale in comparison to Him.[16] The nature of infinity has an interesting quirk: anything less than infinity is, by definition, infinitely less than infinity. You cannot have a portion or a fraction of infinity. Anything finite is infinitely less than something infinite in that same characteristic. By definition, all of the biggest finite numbers ever conceived by human beings, multiplied exponentially into each other, cannot put a dent in infinity. Logically, if we who are finite compare ourselves to God, who is infinite in all of His characteristics, then we become infinitely small, infinitely insignificant, infinitely powerless, and infinitely ignorant by comparison.[17] However, to be "finite", as we humans are, is also to exist. Finite also means "not nothing". In other words, we exist, but only as defined by God. Without Him, we are undefined, without purpose, inconsequential and without eternal value. Our meaning is an extension of His attention to us. Without God, we are - in the big picture - next to nothing.

In all of these characteristics, God is singular.[18] There is no other God.[19] Logically, there cannot be more than one being who overrides all other beings.[20] Two people can share the same knowledge, but two people cannot both have total ruling power over each other. There is no other God. All beings are ultimately subject to the same God.[21] Because God has knowledge of all things and power over all things, He is responsible for all things. To whom is He responsible? Because He is the ultimate judge as well as the original creator, He is responsible to Himself. Everything, including His own decisions, is ultimately subject to His own, perfect judgment. Therefore, all wills, thoughts and intentions, including my will and your will, must ultimately answer to Him and Him alone.

Though He is singular, God is not one-dimensional. God has multiple facets and many aspects of His being just as you and I have many facets of ourselves. Though He is singular in will and in purpose, God's being manifests differently in different circumstances. We are somewhat the same way. For example, a woman can be a mother, a wife, a sister, a friend, a professional, and a daughter all while still existing as a very singular woman. Without compromising her will and her purpose, that same woman might act differently around her husband, her girlfriends, her subordinates at work, her parents, her classmates, or her young child. She might speak in different tones of voice, wear different clothes, discuss different issues, or show affection in different ways between each of those relationships. In other words, she intentionally manifests various aspects of her singular being in order to be able to relate appropriately within different relationships. She can relate on multiple levels without compromising who she is. We humans are that way because God is that way. He made us with personality and characteristics similar to His.

So we come to God's personality. He is more than just a force. There is much more to God than "do" and "do not". God has personality. Because we reflect Him, the nature of His personality is not so different from yours and mine although He is not subject to flaws as we are. God has values. He takes delight in simple things. He is grieved by pain. He empathizes with our suffering. God has an appreciation for beauty and humor - just look at the giraffe to see both at the same time. Without compromising His utter perfection, He has emotions like anger,[22] frustration, and jealousy,[23] in addition to compassion,[24] kindness, love,[25] and affection. Indeed, all of what makes humans good are the very parts of Himself that God planted in our hearts and spirits when He created us. These similarities are what He meant when He said "Let us make man in our image." How wonderful that we as His creation could bear some resemblance to an infinitely perfect Creator! Nonetheless, just as a painting, no matter how wonderful, is not the artist, so we are not God. Indeed, our best qualities are only shadows and reflections of Him. Like shadows, our substance bears no weight against the One we reflect. Even so, He created us such that our hearts are affected by the same matters that affect His heart.

God planted relationships in our hearts because relationships are very important to Him.[26] The best parts of humanity (love, friendship, affection, mercy, kindness) are relational. In healthy relationships we find joy, satisfaction, and peace. Just as we can learn about an artist's personality by looking at his creations, so we can learn about God's personality by looking at His creations.[27] God is relational. And that is where it all begins.

Who is God: Section Summary

- *There is a God. You and I are not God.*
- *To be "God" is to possess all supreme qualities (like supreme origination, omnipotence, omniscience, omnipresence, eternal existence, etc.) in infinite measure.*
- *God cannot possibly make a mistake. Therefore, God's will is perfect and is the origin of every universal "law". Whatever is like God is "right". Whatever violates His will or conflicts with His character is "wrong".*
- *Each of us is ultimately responsible to God according to His will.*

- *God made us. We exist because He wants us to. We are defined in relation to Him.*
- *God has personality. His qualities are reflected in His creations, especially we humans.*

OUR RELATIONSHIP WITH GOD

Our original relationship with God is described in the second and third chapters of Genesis. (If you have not read those two chapters recently and are not closely familiar with what happened to Adam and Eve in the Garden of Eden, take a few minutes to read that short passage of the Bible before you continue reading here. You will understand the upcoming sections of material much better if Adam, Eve, the Serpent, and Eden are fresh in your mind.)

In chapters two and three of Genesis, Adam and Eve, the first man and first woman, learn exactly what it means to be in relationship with their Creator as opposed to being out of relationship with their Creator. Adam and Eve are a case study of God's designed relationship with us as well as our ongoing violation of that design.

Adam and Eve originally had a friend relationship with God that was deep, close and perfect. They were more than just a group of friendly acquaintances: Adam was God's beloved creation and God was Adam's Heavenly Father. God enjoyed His relationship with Adam and Eve. He went out of His way to make sure all of their needs were met. God handcrafted Eve,[1] and Adam rejoiced[2] when he saw the beauty and perfection in God's creation. God took such delight in Adam and Eve that He gave them everything He had made. He placed them over all of His recent creation.[3] Why? Just because! God wanted His beloved to be happy. But He gave them more than that, too.

We humans are well aware that real joy does not result from merely having stuff and comfortable circumstances. Even if you lived in Eden, which had four magnificent rivers, a perfect climate, every good thing to eat, endless variety, inspiring interaction with wildlife, and satisfying work so you would not get bored, all of that would not be much if you were ultimately alone. We humans are designed for relationship. We want significance. We want to be a meaningful part of something larger than ourselves. In that bigger picture, we want to be able to have some choice in the part that we play or at least be able to play it in a way that expresses ourselves. Our relationships do that for us. Healthy relationships are meaningful for everybody involved.

Of course, God has infinite meaning apart from us. Although He does not require us in order to have purpose, He cares for us and desires us to be close to Him. For a human being, the most meaningful relationship of all is the relationship with the One who created us and designed our very purpose around knowing Him. God built a desire for that relationship inside of us because He also wants to have a relationship with His creations. There is no person on earth - past, present, or future – with whom God does not desire[4] to share perfect love, life, purpose, and closeness. God has not created humans who have no meaning to Him.[5]

We can see some aspects of this innate desire for relationship if we look at the way God designed the parent-child relationship. Would you want to have a child who never knew who you are, whose life you could never touch in a meaningful way? If you had a child who was so clearly in your image and had characteristics of you throughout her looks and behavior, would you want that child to benefit from knowing you? Would not that child want to know her father and her mother? Any emotionally honest child who suffers a disconnection from a parent, and any remotely loving parent who suffers a broken relationship with a child can testify that such a rift leaves a gaping hole in life. Nothing can replace a parent-child relationship because we are made to long for it. That longing is there for a reason! Every aspect of your being is carefully crafted. Loving relationships with others are among the best of the gifts He built into us.

Our Creator has specifically given us capacity for many types of love relationships. The parent-child relationship, the sibling relationship, a loving friendship, and the marriage relationship each teach us about different aspects of love. Each of these loving relationships in our earthly lives points directly to the love relationship we are designed to have with our Creator.

In earthly terms, the epitome of a loving relationship is manifested between two committed lovers. Lovers delight in each other's lives. True lovers take joy in the essence of each other's being to the extent that they want to share it… to share being. Lovers want to be as close as possible, even sharing oneness. Eternity is at the heart of true oneness. earthly oneness, or marriage, is intentionally designed to be a single-dimensional reflection of our multi-dimensional relationship with our Creator. Like any good reflection, it is accurate in appearance but different in manifestation. For example, marriage is designed to be eternal in the context of our earthly lives. Our relationship with God is the same way, only much more so because the context is permanent beyond earthly limits. During our earthly lives, we long for a committed life-partner, a life-long friend, with whom to share some kind of oneness in an earthly context. This oneness is a gift from our Creator. He gave us the covenant of marriage as a context in which to enjoy all the benefits of earthly oneness, including sex, which is one of the ultimate expressions of earthly oneness. Of course, in this fallen and sinful world then the covenant is tragically broken and violated. Furthermore, we abuse the privileges of oneness. We twist selflessness into selfishness and cause ourselves much harm in the process. Our Creator designed marriage as a covenant relationship because it allows us a choice of whether or not we enter a lifetime commitment with another person. The marriage commitment is a commitment to oneness until the relationship is broken by death.

God made Adam from dust and placed him in Eden with Eve so that they could see how much their Creator loved them and cared about them. When we humans know we are well-loved, our natural response is to love back.[6] God wanted Adam and Eve to love Him and acknowledge His presence in their lives similar to how a parent wants his children to love him and acknowledge how he loves them. Like a perfect lover, God wanted more than to just be acknowledged and appreciated. He wanted to be forever able to share life with Adam and Eve and to delight in blessing them far beyond simply giving them a terrific garden.

But the nature of any relationship is such that it must be mutual. Nobody can successfully force his way into a genuine love relationship with anybody else. We have the ability to choose not to participate meaningfully in relationships. Real love, the foundation of a satisfying relationship, requires vulnerability. It requires an invitation and mutual participation. Have you ever felt the pain of unrequited love? If so, you know that a loving relationship requires two willing participants.

Enter free will. A relationship is not much without love and love is not much without a free and willing heart. God knew when He created us that the kind of relationship He wants with us would require us to choose to love Him. As the author of love itself, He knows that genuine love requires free will to be authentic and fully engaged if the love is to flourish. Free will cannot necessarily choose whether or not to love or be loved, but we use our wills in choosing if and how we respond to love when it is present. We decide whether to vulnerably invest in that love or to withdraw ourselves and stifle those tendencies. In a legitimate love relationship, either party can weaken the relationship by willfully withholding his or her heart from the other. Openness, trust, selflessness, mutual sacrifice, vulnerability, and loving behavior are all indications that free will is still choosing to support and strengthen the love relationship.

In Eden, Adam and Eve's choice was represented by a tree. The Tree of the

Knowledge of Good and Evil was, in a sense, their way out of Eden if they wanted out. God was not going to confine them to a relationship with Him if they did not want to be with Him. Forced love is no love at all. Although He loves us perfectly, God does not force us to love Him in return. God put many trees in Eden.[7] At the center of the garden stood two special trees. The trees stood in contrast to each other. The first tree was the Tree of Life. The second tree was the Tree of the Knowledge of Good and Evil. God told Adam to feel free to eat from any tree in Eden except for one. If Adam and Eve ate of the Tree of the Knowledge of Good and Evil, then his and her perfect relationships with their Creator would be over: they would "certainly die."[8]

Wait… die? "Obey me or I kill you" does not sound like a loving relationship at all, does it? Of course, God was not making a vindictive threat. Adam's and Eve's relationships with God were not based on threats and coercion but on love and purpose. The Tree of the Knowledge of Good and Evil was not a death threat, at least not as we perceive death threats. After all, Adam and Eve did not even think of death the same way you and I view death. Adam and Eve had never witnessed death before. God had not created a garden full of death and decay because death is not part of God's nature. On the contrary, God is the source of all life. Just as He is the author of love, free will, and beauty, He is also the author of life. Adam was not alive until God breathed life into him.[9] Every living thing in Eden, including Adam and Eve, were extensions of God's infinite life. God is the author and the giver of life. To be with God is to be alive. To have relationship with God is to have life. Accordingly, God was not threatening to kill Adam as a punishment if Adam ate from the tree. God was simply defining what it means to have relationship with God. Relationship with God is life while separation from God is separation from life... meaning death. When we live apart from God, physical death is inevitable because we cannot independently sustain life apart from its source. More importantly, spiritual decay is also inevitable when we our spirit is cut off from the source of its life. If Adam violated the love relationship by eating from the tree, he would be separated from God… separated from life. When God said "If you eat of the tree you will certainly die" He was warning Adam of the natural consequence of rejecting the source of all life. Concerning marriage, "death does us part"; concerning our relationship with our Creator, "in parting do we die."

Our Relationship with God: Section Summary

- *Our significance is a direct function of our relationship with God.*

- *God has wired us for earthly relationships that reflect the eternal relationship He wants with us.*

- *God created us with a genuinely free will. We are able to make a choice to either embrace relationship with Him or reject it.*

- *When we violate and reject God's will, we cannot remain in close relationship with Him. When we choose to exit relationship with God, we are choosing to be cut off from the aspects of Him we do not possess for ourselves, including sustained life.*

- *God is the author and originator of life itself. We cannot sustain life without Him. The moment we are cut off from God, we and all He has given us become subject to death.*

BROKEN RELATIONSHIP AND THE OLDEST LIE IN THE BOOK

Adam understood that choosing to eat of the Tree of the Knowledge of Good and Evil would end, or at least drastically alter, his relationship with God. Eve had the same information. We, Like Adam and Eve, can understand that separation from God is catastrophic because it means we are no longer connected with the only source of real life. Without God, we are as good as dead. We struggle to grasp this death sentence because we have an incomplete concept of death. Our perspective on death is largely a physical perspective. We see a dead deer on the side of the road or we attend a funeral and we understand that the corpse has no more life in it and is already on its way to gross decay. We do not like physical death because it is the ultimate reminder that we are fundamentally not in control. In contrast, God's concept of death is complete. When God told Adam "If you eat of the Tree you will certainly die" then God was not speaking only of physical death. Rather, He was speaking of spiritual death - the unavoidable result of a separation from God. Spiritual death is much more terrifying than physical death.[1] God can breathe life back into a physical body any time He pleases.[2] God breathed life into Adam's body and Eve's body and all the teeming life in Eden with no problems at all. Those lives were permanent so long as they did not break their relationship with God. Do not eat of the Tree. Simple, right?

Unfortunately, it seems that our free will remains contented only as long as it does not start reflecting on itself.[3] Free will, the ability to conceive a desire and to pursue it, bears such striking resemblance to God's omnipotent Will that we are wont to think ourselves quite close to being God. Of course, nothing could be further from the truth. Nevertheless, with a little corruption, our wills all too easily start to covet authority like God's authority. Nobody knew this aspect of free will better than the Devil, who appeared as the Serpent.[4, 5] The Serpent who approached Eve knew exactly how to exploit her free will because he had firsthand experience with corrupted will. A careful study of the Serpent's deception of Eve and Eve's willingness to be deceived can tell us a lot about ourselves, but right now we are primarily concerned with the Serpent's most destructive lie: "You will not certainly die, for God knows that when you eat of it [the Tree] your eyes will be opened, and you will be like God, knowing good and evil."(Genesis 3:4-5)

That lie, "you will not die but you will be like God" remains at the core of every human depravity. The woman ate the fruit because, according to the Serpent's lies, it would enable her to fulfill every level of her desires for herself. She would not be subject to death. After all, God was holding out on her and depriving her of something wonderful, was He not? The fruit would taste good and, much more importantly, she could be like God! Never mind that she was already made in His image and that He had already built His wonderful qualities into her. She wanted to be divine. She wanted supernatural knowledge and special wisdom like she assumed God must have. Then she would no longer need God and His silly rules about not eating the best fruit in Eden. She could be her own god.

The relentless human pursuit of money, sex, power, popularity… they all come back to the same kinds of lies. Though we often know these lies when we hear them, we are still tempted to believe them and live by them. How many of these following lies, or something like them, have stirred up a sense of appeal in you?

> You can be your own God. You will not die.[6] The consequences do not apply to you. You are missing out on something divine! You can be an insider. You do not need God and His silly rules. He is probably just jealous. He is trying to keep you from really living! This is your life. Be your own god. Be the god of the people around

> you. Be appreciated and adored by all who know you! Squash those who would dare fail to properly acknowledge you. You are entitled to whatever you can lay your hands on. You have all the control you want if you simply focus your will! You are the master of your own destiny! You have found "the secret"! Let the desires of your heart guide you. Look inside yourself for the answers! You can rid the world of its ills... if everybody would just listen to you. As for God, if God really loved you He would not be holding out on you. If God loves you then He will want you to do whatever makes you happy, right? Otherwise, you can find your own love. If God cannot love you for who you think you are, for who you really want to be, then forget Him.[7]

Those lies worked in Eden and they still work just as well today. Anything that tells us that we can be some kind of god, that we can develop an independent, self-fulfilling existence, is nothing more than a function of the oldest lie in the Book.[8]

How many of humankind's religions ultimately promise the possibility of making you some kind of god?[9] Whether it is god of your own planet, god of your own paradise, god of the spirit world by disconnecting with the physical world, being eventually reincarnated as a god, or becoming part of the god-force of the universe, these promises are all from the same lies that ruined Adam and Eve. Anything that appeals to our desire for control beyond the control of others, to our desire for control over our total circumstances, or to our desire for unlimited expression of our own self-ness is tapping into that part of us that is so easily exploited to separate us from the one and only true God.[10]

God's nature cannot abide a lie[11] so He cannot abide our attempting to replace Him as God.[12] The heart that does not need God and does not acknowledge His God-ness will suffer a broken relationship with the Creator. When Adam and Eve took of the Tree of the Knowledge of Good and Evil and ate of its fruit, everything changed dramatically... for the worse. Their vulnerability, which had seemed so natural before, suddenly filled them with shame and fear. They hid and tried to cover themselves up. They knew they had been wrong. Instead of asking forgiveness and running to their loving Father, they blamed each other, blamed God, and blamed the Serpent. A heart which blames others and accepts no responsibility for its sin is a heart that is unwilling to participate in relationship. The condition of Adam's heart and Eve's heart was already apparent when they turned from everything God had given them and assumed rule over their own lives by eating the fruit. Because God is established by His perfect nature,[13] they left God with no other option than to separate from them.

Broken Relationship and the Oldest Lie in the Book: Section Summary

- *When it becomes infatuated with its own beauty, free will is easily corrupted into wanting to overrule God Himself and become its own god.*
- *The most ungodly thing we can do is to wish to overrule God's perfect will with our own imperfect will, even in the smallest area of our lives. To do so is to deny that God is God and attempt to replace Him with ourselves. This denial of God's true place and assertion of ourselves is never right.*
- *God cannot embrace contradictions to Himself without violating His own perfection. When we try to replace Him, we are by necessity removed from closeness with Him.*

SEPARATION FROM GOD

Violation of God's perfect will[1] and nonconformity to His perfect nature[2], is called "sin". Is it harsh that a single act of disobedience would lead to a shattering of the most important relationships? Imagine what Adam and Eve must have experienced upon being kicked out of Eden! Their loads of work and pain had been drastically increased for the rest of their lives. Until now, their souls had been fulfilled and happy. They had lacked nothing. Their union with each other and with their Creator had left no holes in their lives. Their existence had been utterly complete. There had been no gaping ache of longing for meaning, significance or companionship. In Eden, they had meaningful purpose and meaningful work. They had been naked and unashamed. God had put Adam and Eve in charge of all lower creation. But now... now death had entered the world. When Adam and Eve sinned, they took the created world, their gift from God, with them. Physical death quickly entered the world in that blood was spilled so that their nakedness could be covered. Spiritual death entered the world because their relationship with God was shattered - He had been their source of true life. Have you or I felt the misery of a terrible argument with a loved one? Have we witnessed the heartbreak of a divorce? Adam and Eve had betrayed each other and betrayed their loving Father. In doing so, they had brought upon themselves divorce from the source of all love, all meaning, and all good. With a single act and a single corruption of their hearts, they stepped from their personalized paradise into a wasteland of decay and aloneness with only remnant memories of what had been before.

Is all that punishment a little much for eating a piece of fruit? We should not be too hasty in saying so. Love-relationships are severely damaged, sometimes irreparably, with a single act of obvious betrayal. To be cut off from God is not some sort of vindictive punishment for sin. Rather, it is the logical result of sin. Adam and Eve were punished for their sin through the specific punishments mandated after their confrontation with God. Eve and her daughters - women - would have pain in childbirth and tension in their relationships with Adam and their husbands. Adam and his sons - men - would henceforth scratch a living from the ground, fight thorns and thistles, and only eat by the sweat of their brows until they returned to dust. The Serpent was also punished for his role in the tragedy.

Adam and Eve's punishments were specifically described. To be banished from Eden and cut off from God is not a punishment, but a consequence. Remember what God had said to Adam about the fruit? Adam would "certainly die" if he ate of the Tree. Death, the spiritual death of being separated from God, was not the punishment for the sin. It was the result of the sin. (Similarly, the punishment for murder is imprisonment while the result of murder is that the victim's life is tragically cut short, which causes much pain and loss to any who loved the victim.) Separation from God, or death, is not merely the punishment but rather an unavoidable consequence of becoming soiled by sin.

In order to best understand why separation from God is the necessary result of sin, then we must remember who God is. We have already covered in the first section that we exist at God's pleasure and that He is all-powerful as well as all-knowing. Consequently, He is perfect in His judgment and unable to make mistakes. We have investigated why His nature defines "right" and anything not of Him is wrong. We understand that He is infinite, singular, and the one to whom all other wills must ultimately bow. In other words, His will is law. We have also examined His authorship of love and His being the source of all life. Additionally, we have developed an appreciation for how He has planted aspects of his personality in our own hearts.

When Adam and Eve embraced unrighteousness then they became, in a word, ungodly. What is ungodly cannot logically be of God because it is, by definition, not of God. Even with the very best of intentions, we still become ungodly the moment we assert our will above God's will. If we choose to be ungodly in our behavior by being unjust, unloving, self-serving, or unrighteous, then we willfully define ourselves apart from God. In other words, the logical consequence of an ungodly heart is to be cut off from God. Adam and Eve's relationship with God, which had begun so beautifully and perfectly, was voluntarily ended. They chose to be separated from God when they chose a path of ungodliness. Because true love relationships require mutual participation, God does not force Himself on us. We can either choose either relationship with Him or separation from Him. Once that choice is made, it is impossible for us to un-make it. God allowed Adam and Eve that choice by making the Tree of the Knowledge of Good and Evil available to them. He told them what would happen if they ate of it. They chose to believe lies instead of believing God. From that moment, nothing was ever the same.

Separation from God: Section Summary

- *Separation from God means separation from everything good and beautiful that He personally fulfilled for us, including significance, meaning, satisfaction with our existence, ongoing life, etc. As a result, we become subject to frustration, decay, and death.*

- *To be cut off from God for voluntarily violating His will with our own will (i.e. to "sin") is not a punishment for sin. Rather, it is a logical result of sin.*

- *If we choose to be ungodly then we willfully define ourselves apart from God. Once that choice is made, it is impossible for us to un-make it.*

OUR POSITION ON A STANDARD OF RIGHTEOUSNESS

If you were afraid this was all going to get personal then you were right. Because God is eternal and does not change, the same circumstances apply to us as applied to Adam and Eve. Our relationship with God was broken from birth because we, like every generation since Adam and Eve, were born into ungodliness. God had placed Adam and Eve in authority over much of His creation. Simply put, when Adam and Eve drove themselves into sin, they took their offspring and the whole created world with them. Even if we had been born into righteousness, as Adam and Eve were, we have made choices that result in our separation from God, just as they did. Every one of us would have been necessarily banned from Eden.

It is important that we understand what "righteousness", rectitude, or being "right" means, exactly. God's very nature defines righteousness. We rightly perceive this righteousness as an omnipotently enforced "law" of right versus wrong. God enforces that law because it perfectly reflects the most important and most fundamental truth in the entire universe: there is one perfectly supreme Being in all existence - you are not Him. Righteousness describes conformity to that truth.

The core of sin and unrighteousness is denial of God's rightful supremacy. To disobey God is to assert that "self" is more worthy than God. Such an assertion is at the heart of all sin. When we lie, we assert that truth, which is an elemental aspect of God's nature, is somehow less important than our immediate comfort in our circumstances. When we gossip, we place ourselves above others, as though we have made ourselves better than others God has made. To place "self" in preference to the Being that is rightfully God is an utter desecration of the actual reality within which we exist. Because each human being includes an eternal spirit, and because reality cannot be indefinitely denied, we must ultimately answer to reality.

Every one of us has deliberately broken God's standard of perfect righteousness. We have each made unrighteous decisions. As we are compared to God's perfect standard, failure in a single area effectively is failure in every area.[1]

Does something in us churn uncomfortably as we contemplate these thoughts? It is an uncomfortable truth to realize we are on the wrong side of a law much larger than ourselves.[2] Because of our separation from God, our nature is fallen from a righteous standard. We do not conform to the most important truth in the universe. In willful disobedience, we have foolishly acted as though we are greater than God. We can expect a reminder of that truth to be uncomfortable.

You and I know that good relationships often require overlooking shortcomings. So we might ask ourselves, "If God is so loving, why doesn't He forgive us? After all, isn't He the one who created us in His own image? How can we help it if we get a little confused and mistake ourselves for God? If He wants a relationship with us, and if we are flawed from birth, will He not overlook our imperfections?" He will not because He cannot. First, just as it is cruel for a parent to neglect a child, it would be cruel for God to allow us to go on harming ourselves. His recognition of sin and discouragement of further sin are His loving guidance in our lives. More importantly, God cannot ignore sin because sin is anti-God. God cannot ignore sin without compromising the core of His nature. God is perfect, pure, and good through and through. Sin is everything that is detestable, filthy, and ugly. Although we were designed and intended for cleanliness, we used our free will to stray from our Creator's intent for us. As a result, we are riddled with sin. We are not simply infected, it is in our spiritual DNA.[3] His nature of perfect righteousness will not allow Him to embrace an iota of sin.[4] We are marred with sin and all of its repugnance. Unless we can somehow be rid of sin and its effects on us, we cannot expect our all-seeing creator to feign blindness and pretend that our sin is somehow a non-issue.

These standards may sound harsh but if we set our indignation aside then we will realize that a standard of perfection the only way righteousness can be fulfilled. Could you imagine a God who was willing to simply ignore occasional sins? Would you want anything to do with a God who would only enforce justice arbitrarily or on some sliding scale? When God considers a person's heart, He cannot arbitrarily call what is wrong "right" or He would be disqualified to judge. True justice is not enforced on a curve. Even the best of intentions do not make up for unrighteous actions. A just judge must always enforce the law. God's universal law as it results from His nature - the very parameters of righteousness - is a perfect standard.

Sadly, a humanist view of God in which we demand to be embraced, filthiness and all, is frequently carried like a banner by people who reject God's intent for their lives. You might have heard (or thought) something like: "My sins, if you want to call them that, really aren't so bad. If God doesn't agree with me and isn't willing to overlook our differences then He's no god of mine." Fortunately for the sake of true righteousness, such an argument is flawed. First, it replaces God's perfect standard of righteousness with our own, self-serving, mutation of "right".[5] Second, it is logically impossible for God to embrace into Himself something that is in blatant violation of His nature. He cannot accept sin as part of Himself because sin is, by definition, ungodliness. Finally, arbitrary justice is one of the worst forms of corruption. A moving standard is no standard at all. Wavering justice which holds to no true standard will ultimately defeat itself. If God ignored even one sin then how could He be just or fair in punishing any sin at all? Taken to an extreme, such reasoning could not justify punishing even the worst sins imaginable. Where would it be "right" to draw an arbitrary line? The entire system of justice and righteousness would be worthless. The God we thought we knew would have turned out to be nothing more than a cruel trickster who makes unreasonable demands only because He can. We can be glad this is not the case!

Keep in mind this important distinction when it comes to "your will" and "God's will": violation of God's will happens in matters of morality and righteousness. God's will is usually not difficult to anticipate. When it is difficult, He will help us if we ask Him and pay attention to His answer. In questions of mere preference, where righteousness is not at stake and your decisions are not causing pain to others, you do not usually profit by agonizing over what God's will might be. For example, righteousness is usually not at stake in deciding what kind of sandwich to have for lunch. Similarly, the color of socks you choose is generally a matter of preference, not a matter of sin. Beware of people who say otherwise! God gives us freedom in many decisions, even big ones. A graduating high school student making a college decision may unnecessarily drive herself into a frenzy in agonizing over whether it is "God's will" for her to attend Duke versus Notre Dame. All else equal, God's will usually aligns with practicality, wisdom, and peace. In other words, you do not need to fear inadvertently violating God's will when one choice is not clearly more righteous or morally correct than the other. If you are not acting selfishly, being divisive, or making an obvious moral blunder, use your God-given judgment to make a reasonably good choice. The real problems begin when you do not bother to ask God for His input or, worse yet, when you already know in your heart what is right but you readily talk yourself out of it. Our violation of righteousness is not by not knowing things we do not and cannot know. Rather, we violate righteousness when, even for an instant, we willfully ignore what we know to be right.

God's perfection is comforting when we long for justice, but that same standard dismays us because we were designed for close relationship with Him. Now that we have willingly chosen ourselves over Him, we are lost and without purpose. We who are imperfect desire to be embraced by a heavenly Father who is obligated to enforce perfect standards with perfect consistency. Anything less would be imperfect. On our own, none of us lives up to that standard.

We know we are rightly separated from God as soon as we examine our own hearts and realize that our hearts are different than God's heart.[6] Every instance in which you or I have willfully blocked God from any area of our lives, we embraced ungodliness. Just as an adulterous husband or wife cannot undo the betrayal he or she embraced, we cannot undo our ungodliness. When we voluntarily separate from God who is our true life, we cannot, on our own merit, voluntarily enter again into relationship with Him as though we had never sinned. Hence, unless we are rescued, we live subject to death and decay.

Our hearts are subject to selfishness, greed, lust, bitterness, envy, and all sorts of ungodly attitudes. We war against ourselves to try and make righteous decisions. Every one of us has fallen victim to the lies in Eden, especially the oldest lie in the Book. As relationships are not solely defined by actions but also by the heart,

God looks at the affections of our hearts to see where our love lies. He does not have to look far. A heart that has lusted is an adulterous heart. A heart laced with hatred is, by His standard, a murderous heart. A heart that has lied is a heart that is in line with the Serpent's heart rather than God's heart. We know what is in our hearts by our actions and by our words. There is not a person on the planet who, by evidence of his words and actions, has not chosen over and over to embrace self and further ungodliness instead of a relationship with his Creator. We were born outside of Eden. Everything we do in and of ourselves drives us further into the wilderness outside of a relationship with our Creator.

Our Position on a Standard of Righteousness: Section Summary

- *Righteousness, rectitude or "being right" describes perfect accordance with the most important universal truth: there is a supreme God of the universe and you are not Him. Any time we place our own will in direct opposition to God's will, we sin. Sin occurs in matters of righteousness and morality, not in matters of mere preference where God has given us freedom to choose according to our own will.*

- *We as humans are corporately and individually under sin. We are all separated from God. We continue to use our wills to make choices that violate His perfect will.*

- *As much as He wants relationship with us and as much as we are better off in relationship with Him, God cannot simply ignore our constant violations of "right" in the name of forgiveness.*

- *Once we have voluntarily placed "self" above God, we cannot, on our own merit, enter into closeness with Him as though we had never sinned. As a result, we are subject to death and decay. Our only hope is to be somehow rescued.*

FORGIVENESS VS. JUSTICE

God was not surprised when Adam and Eve, His beloved creations, chose to end their relationships with Him. God is never surprised because His ability to know and determine outcomes is perfect. So why did He create humankind in the first place if He knew that we would stray from Him? There is, really, only one possible answer. If we know that God makes no mistakes then we can assume that creating humankind was the best and right thing to do in spite of humankind's decision to stray from Him. Since we know God did not create us humans to waste away and be doomed to eternal separation from Him, we can be certain the He is not finished. Because He does not make mistakes, God must have some way of reconciling us to Himself.

In our human relationships, reconciliation usually begins with forgiveness. Our natural inclination is to wonder why God cannot simply forgive us. It would seem that somebody who cared so much would be more than willing to overlook our flaws and welcome us gladly home. Between humans, this sort of forgiveness demonstrates a heart of love, which reflects God's own love. It would be foolish for me to hold something against you when I am no better than you at all. It is not my position to judge you or to hold you accountable to God's standard of justice. However, what if I was in a position that demanded me to treat you according to your merit against a strict standard of righteousness and justice? For example, our legal systems have judges who are expected to measure out justice. A good judge cannot forego justice for the sake of forgiveness. If he did, the law would mean nothing and he would be failing his role of judging according to a standard of justice.

One of the strongest traits we have in common with our Creator is an intense appreciation for righteousness and justice.[1] Although we, unlike our Creator, fall well short of those standards, we know them when we see them. Our blood boils when we have been treated unfairly. Even small children quickly learn to shout "That's not fair!" and parents will quickly to respond to the effect of "Life is not fair, so deal with it!" Yet we loathe dealing with life's injustices because we know that injustice is wrong. Sometimes it is ok with us when life is unfair in our favor, but the lone survivor among victims of a plane crash can testify that we even attach some guilt to the more pleasant side of injustice. We have a problem with injustice because justice is right. It is wrong to be unjust. Even as children we understand that justice and righteousness are inextricably linked. Righteousness demands justice. They are the two dimensions, two perfect standards, which define morality.

A craving for justice is part of what makes us human. God put that desire there because justice is an irrefutable element of His nature. The part of God's nature that assures justice is perhaps the most comforting part of His nature for us who impatiently exist in an unjust world.[2] Remember how all wills, thought and intentions, including my will and your will, must ultimately answer to Him and Him alone? On what basis do they answer? Do they answer according to the Creator's abstract whim? Is God's judgment measured out with reckless abandon or random condemnation? Of course not. On the contrary, God is the ultimate just Judge. His nature defines righteousness and His judgments define justice. God cannot logically violate His own nature. He cannot be what He is not, nor can He act how He does not act. He cannot have poor judgment when He has perfect knowledge, perfect power, and perfect understanding. Accordingly, God's justice is the justice by which all other justice is measured. Every being is ultimately held accountable to His standard of justice and righteousness.

Let us dig into this concept of justice versus forgiveness with a hypothetical example. In this example, you own a very rare car. It's a one-of-a-kind vehicle with tremendous historical value as well as sentimental value. This vehicle, if you were to sell it at an auction, would command tens of millions of dollars. In our example, you have to leave town for a while so you temporarily entrust me with the safekeeping and guardianship of your car. Instead of caring for your priceless car as I said I would, I promptly take the vehicle joyriding. My reckless joyride ends when I careen through several red lights at top speed and subsequently collide with a city bus. The accident causes injuries to some of the bus passengers and totals your car beyond all hope of repair. As the car was a convertible, I am thrown clear of the vehicle and, luckily for me, I land in a lake where I swim to shore unharmed and am promptly arrested. Unfortunately, your insurance will not cover the event.

What would you expect when I am brought before the local judge? It is his job to uphold justice. Surely I must be punished. Would it be right for the judge to, in the name of mercy, simply say "I forgive the offender. Court adjourned."? Of course not. You would be furious and rightly so! Your car cannot be restored to you and you did not receive acceptable recompense for your loss. The judge's forgiveness, in this case, violates justice. Unless the traffic violations are paid, the injuries are recovered, a new bus purchased for the city, and the value of your property is fully restored to you, it cannot be just for me as an offender to simply go free and enjoy all the privileges of a law-abiding citizen. If the judge holds himself to any standard of justice, he had better come up with an improved solution.

What if the judge ordered me to pay my fines and pay you for the damaged property? I could never come up with an amount that would be anything but insulting to the value of your car, not to mention the injuries I caused to the bus passengers. The only remaining penalty for not paying my debts is prison, which is long-term separation from upstanding society. By my inability to pay for my lawlessness, I would have violated my obligation to society to the extent that I would have to be cut off from society. Yet, even if I were placed in jail for a very long time, my punishment would be vaguely "just" but it would not restore your car or pay you for the damage. As humans who live in a broken, unjust world, this last solution - separation - is often the closest semblance of justice we can enforce.

A perfect solution would pay entirely for the damage to your property, take care of the bus passengers, restore the bus, and pay the fines for my traffic violations. Furthermore and perhaps most importantly, a perfect solution would have me demonstrate a changed heart to the extent that you and the rest of society are satisfied enough to forgive me for my crimes and welcome me back into society. Unfortunately, the debt is far too great for me to bear[3] even if I desperately wanted to try and repay it. Perfect justice would be completely beyond my means.

There is only one possible, though unlikely, option for total forgiveness and justice: somebody with the means to do so could volunteer to pay my debt for me. That benefactor would have to justify the losses with major financial compensation. I would have to accept the benefactor's generous gift of paying my fines on my behalf. Additionally, I would have to demonstrate a dramatically changed heart and repent of my crimes in order to be restored to society. With this substitution method of justice, the debt is paid, justice is served, and I am kept from wasting away in prison as a "just" but impotent solution.

Is that solution of somebody else paying my debt a fair solution? No. It satisfies justice, but at great cost to somebody. Justice is much bigger than mere equality and it is much deeper than simply being "fair". The nature of forgiveness for the sake of justifying a debt is that it costs somebody something. Forgiveness is never free to everybody involved. That benefactor would have to dearly love me to intercede on my behalf at such great cost to him or herself. Wherever a debt is forgiven, somebody somewhere absorbs the cost. If there is no significant debt, whether monetary, social, legal, or emotional, then there would be nothing to forgive. If you forgive your neighbor, you absorb the cost of some debt he has to you. You and I can do that for our neighbors because we are not in a position requiring us to enforce justice against them. God, however, is obligated by His nature to uphold justice according to His law of righteousness. His solutions must fulfill justice perfectly, at any cost, because His actions define perfection.

Much as He would love to be able to simply reconcile our relationship with Him without punishing our sin, God faces two major problems: First, as the One responsible for enforcing justice according to His righteous nature, failing to punish sin would violate justice and righteousness. Second, even if justice is served, a just punishment does not remove us from "ungodly" status. When we chose sin we became "not of God". Until that problem is solved, He must remain separated from us and we are appropriately imprisoned by our choices in an existence separated from the source of life. Thus, while God dwells in heaven, we are surrounded by death and decay as we cling to whatever tokens of life and beauty we can find.

- *Because God must have foreseen our choices to ruin ourselves, He must also have foreseen how He would be able to redeem us from our predicament. Anything less would be unloving on His part.*

- *God is responsible for enforcing the law of "right" as defined by His nature. His nature demands that "wrong" is appropriately punished. If He simply ignored sin and embraced everybody as though they were inherently acceptable then God would be as corrupt as a judge who did not enforce the law.*

- *Justice and Righteousness are inextricably linked. They are foundational to God's perfect judgment.*

- *In strictly human terms, a "just" punishment for wrong may still fail to restore the losses resulting from the crime.*

- *Our debts to righteousness are so great that our only hope is that a loving benefactor will intercede on our behalf so that we do not have to be eternally cut off from righteous society like imprisoned criminals.*

- *As the ultimate just judge, God's forgiveness cannot be at the expense of righteousness and justice.*

- *We cannot restore ourselves to righteousness and God cannot rightly overlook our sin.*

Furthermore, we do not have the means to pay appropriately for our sin in order to satisfy the law.

PROTOCOL

When a relationship is broken the protocol will change. A husband and wife who go through a heart-wrenching divorce might develop a new dynamic in their shattered relationship. For a time, if they interact at all, that new dynamic will be civil at best, but little else. There are barriers now. The openness and vulnerability that originally made the relationship so delightful are now gone. Sometimes legal agreements are reached that allow a parent to see a child or former spouse only so often and at certain times while under specific circumstances. Unless those rules are followed, the parent and child are unable to have any relationship at all. Two parties of what was once an intimate and special relationship may act like strangers even though they probably know each other better than anybody else on the planet. Their relationship has changed and only a miracle can restore it.

Our broken relationship with our Creator is not so different. When we made choices resulting in our separation from Him then protocols had to be put in place in order for us to have any interaction with Him at all. God relentlessly pursues a relationship with us. We can be sure that He gives us every opportunity to know Him so that we will not choose to be eternally isolated from Him. However, because of the sin barrier between us and God, He was obligated to place strict protocols on the relationship. These protocols allowed limited interaction where there would otherwise have been no interaction at all. These rules temporarily allowed us to still be involved with our Creator even though He had every reason to treat us as enemies.[1]

We can see this post-Eden protocol developed and recorded in the first several books of the Bible. It is a set of laws which describe exactly how and in what manner we could acknowledge our sin and temporarily address it in order to approach our Creator. In addition to providing a means by which our broken relationship could still limp along, the laws also revealed to us a lot about God and showed us how He views sin. The extreme difficulty in abiding by the laws, even for the most dedicated followers, reminds us that we are ultimately subject to God's mercy if we want to avoid permanent isolation. Though God did interact with humanity through the old laws, the purpose of those laws (sometimes called the Old Testament laws, the Mosaic Covenant, or the Torah) was not to eternally restore us to God.[2] Rather, those laws were put in place by God to help us understand the extent of our sinful predicament.[3] Those laws highlight God's perfection in the context of our own corrupted state.[4] As a result, we get a better grasp on the depth of our need for God's mercy.[5]

Among other requirements, the laws required that God was approached on the basis on sacrifice. God was not asking for sacrifice because He takes pleasure in animal blood. Rather, the picture was for our sake. Sacrifice helps bring our hearts to a condition in which we put ourselves aside and can know God better. In the Bible, those relationship protocols required that a relationship with God be taken very seriously. Indeed, an entire culture revolved around trying to restore some semblance of a relationship with Him. The complex system of blood sacrifices required after the fall of Eden had a four-fold purpose. First, sacrifices drove home the expectation that sin results in death[6] and requires bloodshed. Second, the law reminded us that we are facing punishment for our ungodliness and that we desperately need forgiveness for our sin.[7] Third, the law provided a means by which a portion of society, the priesthood, could focus full-time on turning the hearts of the people to their Creator and representing the people to Him. Fourth and most importantly, the post-Eden system of blood sacrifices set the stage for the means by which God would enable a total reconciliation of fallen humanity to Himself.[8]

Protocol: Section Summary

- *The first portion of the Old Testament (or the Torah) in the Bible outlines a set of temporary laws God put in place in order to have some partial relationship with His beloved people. Those laws were a system by which sin could be symbolically addressed and the people under that law could symbolically approach God.*

- *Those laws were put in place by God to help us understand the extent of our sinful predicament. Because nobody could perfectly follow it, the system could not restore us to perfect godliness. The old system was neither intended nor able to restore us to perfect godliness.*

- *The "old law" system reflected God's plan for ultimately restoring us to Himself. God's forthcoming plan for full restoration replaces and fulfills the old law system.*

A WORLD APART FROM OUR CREATOR

The depravity of our world is blunt testimony to why our relationship with our Creator matters. The world in its current state[1] is separated from Him by necessity of His nature. We dreadfully miss being in Eden, where we enjoyed all the benefits[2] of having a close relationship with a Creator who loves us and is also the most powerful being in the universe.

Though many people do not know exactly why the world is the way it is, everybody recognizes that something is wrong. We see sickness, death and decay[3] all around us. We are not made to coexist with these conditions. Indeed, both individually and as a race, we all ultimately fall victim to all three of them... and we know it is not right.

Pain, suffering, and sickness are indications that something is wrong. When we have searing abdominal pain we go to the doctor and say "Something is wrong!" The same is true on a larger scale. No reasonable doctor would say that debilitating cancer is a good and natural progression in a healthy life. No bereaved mother gives birth to a stillborn child without feeling a staggering sense of loss.

No matter the explanations, she knows in her heart of hearts that babies are not meant to be stillborn. Something is wrong with this world. We know that all this suffering does not belong among us, but the harder we try the worse it gets. Is there any solution? The best we can hope for is death by old age, yet we fear even old age because we recognize it as a state of decay. Why should age kill us anyway? Our world is so off-kilter that, even under the best of circumstances, it seems almost no human can survive a 120-year stay. Much of the global population would be lucky to even live half so long before they succumb to sickness, decay, death, and subsequently, more decay. Is this really how we were created to live... to die? Are we meant to consistently fight a battle in which our greatest hope is to lose more gracefully than the previous generation - and we are unlikely to achieve even that low bar for success?

We are stuck in a place of exhaustion and decay[4]. We are exhausted because we are disconnected from our source of energy and life. We decay because, being disconnected from life, we are dreadfully subject to a lifetime of hurtling towards eternal death with the whole world for company but only one's self for comfort.

It gets worse. Besides simply losing the struggle against sickness, death, and decay, humanity as a whole struggles in the most depraved fashion.[5] We inflict our worst fears on the people around us, even those we love. We know there is a beauty in unity but we are only likely to unify temporarily and in the name of self-preservation or self-promotion. Entire societies and systems of life are based on achieving safety by oppressing others. We live like we are in constant terror of being rejected by those we would willingly deny in order to save ourselves.[6]

Look at how we treat each other! Who has not inflicted pain in the life of another? Who has not, at times, done so intentionally? Who among us has not wished even for a moment for catastrophe, disaster, or suffering to befall another human being or group of human beings? Every generation knows how to hate war and still every generation has demonstrated its ability to expertly wage the very thing it hates. What category of sin is not rampant in some or all corners of the globe? How many civilizations have not had to defend themselves against some other civilizations bent on their destruction? On an individual level, who among us has not suffered as a result of the sin of others? Who is not familiar with the pain of betrayal, isolation, backstabbing, neglect, broken promises, shattered trust, or some form of abuse? We justify our worst actions by saying the other is even worse than we are. No wonder the best evidence most of us can give of being a "good" person is "Well I've never murdered anybody."

Then, when we cannot take it any longer, we give in to self-destruction. Alcohol abuse, illicit drugs, ruinous relationships, perverted and destructive sexuality, gluttony, prescription drug abuse, substance abuse, brazen cynicism, bitterness, hatred, mockery, every flavor of greed… we work ourselves to death, we spend our lives running from the shadows of our pasts, we seek every form of distraction, every form of entertainment, every form of self-indulgence at any expense, we run away from our pain and, in the process, find new ways to create more of it. Occasionally we can hole up in some cave of fragile peace but eventually we find ourselves all but ready to welcome death. Some of us will even inflict it upon ourselves. Our most comforting thought is that death will at least bring nothingness which really must be better than all this somethingness. Is this really the life for which we were created?[7]

Maddeningly, there are the parts of ourselves that we know are good but we cannot seem to successfully manifest.[8] Nobody in his right mind enters a marriage while aspiring to be a crummy spouse, yet marriages everywhere are broken or floundering. Nobody has children with the hope of damaging them, yet so many of us grow up and spend the rest of our lives coming to terms with aspects of our childhoods. We have desires, good desires, to contribute in a positive way to the lives around us. We do not want to waste our lives in the rat race. We want to, as Thoreau said, "to live deliberately, to live deeply and suck all the marrow out of life". We work hard trying to arrange our lives accordingly and then we pause midway, reflect on our largely empty efforts, and say "is this all there is?" So we buy new toys, cheat, leave our spouses, escape into the internet, and throw ourselves headlong back into our work or maybe some new, "better" lover. Through it all, we have this feeling that we are created for something bigger. We want true relationship and meaning but our most constant friends are Isolation and Emptiness. Once upon a time, as children, we once had an expectation that life would offer some kind of lasting satisfaction.

Life does have elements of satisfaction. We take delight in a job well done, in simple beauty, or in healthy relationships. Those joys are all remnants of the Image in which we were created. Yet we are in a hopeless position without our Creator.[9] Without our Creator, we become myopic, turned inward, and determined to become gods of our own existences. Our Creator is the source of life and every good thing. Because we are separated from Him, our lives are stymied and our good characteristics are distorted. Our human nature is completely lost without Him so we are constantly trying to get back to Him through use or misuse of the world He created for us. Sadly, even in our best efforts we typically try to reach Him on our own terms. This effort is generally known as "religion". Religion in and of itself is little more than organized behavior. Some aspects of religion are helpful in removing distractions or helping us understand God's nature more clearly. Nevertheless, no religion, however faithfully followed, has ever succeeded in fully reuniting sinful men with God. Organized behavior is a poor substitute for true relationship. Indeed, we are closer to Him if we follow the relationship protocols (the laws) that He laid down for us. Persistently, those laws chafe against our selfish nature. Like children, we blame Him for our problems. We think, "If He really loves us then why will He not forget those useless laws and just meet us on our own terms!" We become angry that the God of the universe will not compromise His nature for our convenience. In other words, we forget that He is God and we are not. Consequently, we wander further from Him than ever. Just like Eve in Eden we suspect that He is holding out on us and we wish we could become gods too, or even instead.

He is not holding out on us like some arrogant, out of touch deity. Does not a loving father suffer to see His children turn to mutual destruction and blame Him? How much more does our broken life in this world grieve the One who created us in His own image and said "it is good!" when He finished? Like any loving father, God is angered by our sin and rebellion but He is also grieved by our pain.[10] Like rebellious children, we perceive His anger but we cannot fathom His pain. Our pride has us rebelling more than ever to the point of denying His very existence unless we personally arrive at rock bottom. Only then do we cry out to Him. If our personal discomfort is really bad then we may even be willing to make a few temporary concessions of our own if only He will fix our current circumstances.

God does not want our half-hearted promises to be good. He knows that we will break those promises anyway, usually by the end of the week. He is not merely interested in our attending church, giving to a charity, or quitting a bad habit. Those things are nice, even good, but little more: they do not effectively address our core problems. Behavior modification does not repay our debt to a law of righteousness. In the same way, it was not the blood of the sheep and goats that pleased Him under the old protocol.[11] The God of the universe is interested in the condition of our hearts.[12] He loves us perfectly and He wants us to love Him wholeheartedly. Our Creator is delighted when we actively acknowledge our longing for a relationship with Him. Until we realize our deep and ultimate need for our Heavenly Father,[13] until we throw ourselves at His mercy and express true, unbridled sorrow for our sin and rebellion, we will continue to wallow in our own self-created depravity apart from the only One who can rescue us, meet our needs, and fulfill our deepest desires for significance, purpose, relationship, and love.

A World apart from Our Creator: Section Summary

- *So long as we are cut off from God, we are maddeningly subject to sickness, death and decay. We flounder to find our purpose without God.*
- *Our own depravity continues to get the best of us even when we try to improve ourselves.*
- *We suffer tragically because of the pervasive sin in the world.*
- *Because He loves us, God is deeply grieved to see the suffering we insist on inflicting on ourselves and on others.*
- *Behavior modification does not fix our problems. God is interested in our behavior only as it reflects our hearts. What we need is heart modification. We cannot modify our own hearts.*

HELL AND HEAVEN

Had enough? If this is all starting to feel somewhat overwhelming then you are on the right track to understanding the magnitude of the situation we face as we have broken our relationship with our Creator. As sad as this world can sometimes feel during honest reflection, we have not yet addressed the most important part of all: eternity.

The God who created us is an eternal being. He is infinite in His nature and His existence. He has built eternity into us. We exist beyond our physical death. Our hearts in this life determine whether we can be eternally united with our loving Creator or, alternatively, live apart from Him forever.[1] There is a word for final, eternal separation from God: Hell.

To be completely, entirely, permanently cut off from God is to be cut off from all life,[2] all love, all goodness, all light, and all redeeming qualities. Furthermore, without God, the most beautiful characteristics of Himself that He so carefully planted in you, including meaningful relationships, wholesome interactions, the ability to edify another, will quickly succumb to the most depraved aspects of human nature. So much for the empowerment of self-actualization. Hell is where you are left to turn infinitely into your own, debased self… with no way out.[3] Hell is where everything right with this world is absent while everything wrong with this world increases into infinity. Nothing good survives or is sustained outside of God. Absolute Hell is where God absolutely is not. The creative source of all good, God, is has no presence in Hell. As a result, nothing in Hell provides a foundation, an orientation, an iota of satisfaction or progress towards anything remotely good or new. Hell is where you are unfathomably alone, unredeemed, and excruciatingly isolated from even the faintest semblance of what had ever brought you comfort.[4] In Hell, everything for which you were so beautifully designed is now utterly impossible. Hell is where your nightmares overcome you, not necessarily because they are being intentionally inflicted upon you but because there is nothing to stop them... without God you are an oh-so fertile ground for nightmares. Evil can finally have its way with you.[5] In Hell you flounder in unattached nothingness while, in the absence of all light, true darkness smothers you. There is no gasp of sweet, life-giving air because there is no life to give.[6] Your every frantic, twitching effort increases the crushing weight of existing eternally apart from the God who so desperately wanted you to be in Paradise with Him. But in Hell, it is too late. Hell is an eternal sentence. You embraced your own self as god and you rejected the One True God over and over. You tried to replace Him with yourself and you have permanently succeeded. Congratulations: yourself is all you have. What did you expect?

Every day you are on earth you have the opportunity to turn to God. Hell is what happens after you reject Him for the last time.[7] Your free will can string you along, moment by moment and day by day, to your own eternal destruction. You are not banished to Hell because God gleefully inflicts Hell on you, but because, if you insist on rejecting Him, He will ultimately let you have your way.[8]

If Hell is the place where God is not, Heaven is the place where we are most in His presence.[9] Heaven is the inverse of Hell because Heaven is where nothing increases in opposition to God. In Heaven, we will find an infinity of purpose, love, joy, peace, understanding, vitality, and hope. Heaven is not just where good things live, it is the place from which good originates. It is where the presence of God is palpably, joyfully, uninhibited.

Just as Hell is the eternal manifestation of our consistently rejecting God, Heaven is the eternal manifestation of God's restoring us to Him. In other words, they are destinations. We do not "earn" Hell any more than we earn an airport by getting off an airplane. Similarly, we do not earn our way into Heaven because nothing we do could possibly qualify us to spend eternity in God's perfection. The road to Hell was built by human hands and paved with the desires of humankind. The path to Heaven is God's loving mercy.[10]

Hell and Heaven: Section Summary

- *Hell is real. It is the inevitable consequence of being cut off from God.*

- *While we live this life on earth then we are partially cut off from God but we have His continuing efforts and hope of possible restoration. Because He wants us to return to Him, God is actively engaged with us on earth. If we are in Hell, He is infinitely, permanently, removed from our lives... forever.*

- *We are ultimately eternal beings and will either be eternally with God or eternally without Him. Hell is a final decision. It is an eternal condemnation to being left with ourselves and having nothing whatsoever to do with God or the goodness only He can supply and sustain.*

- *God does not want to send anybody to Hell. Rather, we choose Hell largely out of our willful ignorance. God is willing to ultimately honor our free will even if we continue to reject Him and insist on being apart from Him.*

- *Heaven is also a real place. It is where we are eternally in God's presence and enjoy the benefits of spending eternity in uninhibited perfection, purpose, and joy.*

- *We make our way to Hell by refusing to rightfully acknowledge God. We can be in Heaven only by God's mercy because we cannot earn His presence.*

NATURAL CONSEQUENCES AND THE DEVIL'S ROLE

Let us take just moment to review the differences between Debt and Punishment. Sin results in punishment, or consequences. Adam and Eve, for example, were mandated specific consequences for their specific sins in the Garden of Eden. We see consequences of sin around us all the time and every day. Sin results in death,[1] incapacitation, loss, apathy and suffering. Sin destroys. It eclipses what is good and it causes much pain both to those who commit the sin and to those who are in the proximity of sin. Similarly, righteousness has its rewards. Righteousness in relationships results in wholesome and meaningful relationships. Righteous living directly contributes to a more peaceful life with fewer problems and more long-term satisfaction. The reality we know reflects a truth bigger than human convenience: it is better to follow God's idea of right than to rule one's own life apart from God's standards. We call this reality "natural consequence". Even if we wished natural consequences did not exist, there is little we can do about them. Nevertheless, because this world is so marred and corrupted by sin, because we have insisted that we be rulers of our world instead of submitting to the true God, the reward/consequence system is also corrupted.

Our corrupted world with its skewed system of natural consequences is very much influenced by the Devil. The Devil himself is the patient mentor of any world that wishes to be its own god. Notice that the Devil - who was working through the Serpent[2] in the Garden of Eden - did not have to convince Adam and eve to worship the Devil instead of God. No, the Devil is crafty enough to know that the moment we turn from the true God, we are with the Devil by default. There are only two categories that matter in the long run: "Friends of God", who will be eternally with God; and "Enemies of God" who will be eternally separated from God. When we become enemies of God by trying to replace Him with ourselves, we are safely in the category where the Devil has his way. Once we choose to be enemies of God, as we have all voluntarily chosen at many points, we cannot return to friendship with Him of our own capacity .

The Devil lies to us in order to corrupt us from truth. When we believe and follow lies, we play fiddle for him without even realizing it. We do not even have to know or believe that the Devil exists in order to conform to what he wants us to do with our time on this earth.[3] Think of it this way: if God is the maestro conductor of a divine orchestra and we are the individual musicians, the Devil can ruin the music by having us play anything but the correct notes at the correct time. The Devil's composition is chaos. He makes determined efforts to destroy whatever good God has made. The Devil does not have to convince us to understand, believe in, or willingly play his composition. If he can quietly convince the musicians that notes of one's own choosing are more personally fulfilling than the notes on the page, the Devil's strategy of confusion and chaos will play out exactly as he wants it. If the Devil can get us to turn from God and be eternally cut off from our Creator, then the Devil will have the rest of eternity to work with us according to his own desires.

You and I are made in God's image.[4] When God made us, He said "it is good!" The Devil destroys what is good. The Bible calls the Devil a murderer, a liar, and a destroyer.[5] In other words, the Devil hates you and he hates me. He is methodically, scrupulously, deliberately devoted to your utter destruction. He is more than happy to use chaos, confusion, and distraction to destroy your chances of being reconciled to your Creator. Just as he did to Eve in the Garden of Eden, the Devil will tap into your free will and whisper whatever cajoling lies necessary in order to turn our worship inwards to ourselves rather than turning towards God. In full bloom, the consequences are as potent as though we had knowingly chosen to worship the Devil himself.

There is something very important that we should notice about the Devil's role. Satan has a two-fold, yet singular, purpose in our lives: to turn us from God and to be sure that we do not return to Him. There is a common misconception that the Devil is spending all of his time trying to get people to do bad things. Does he really have to? We do bad things on our own. Once we are off-course, Satan does not benefit from making us go further off-course so much as he desires to make sure we never return to the correct course. For this reason, Satan attacks the truth. He distorts it at every possible opportunity so that we who are corrupted will not easily understand God's plan to restore us to Himself.[6]

By giving ourselves over to sin, we have taken the world into dark hands. As a result, sin and righteousness are not perfectly punished and rewarded. Innocent people suffer because the world has wrenched itself from under God's perfect system into confusion, corruption and chaos. Many people reject God because they say, "If there is a God, then why do bad things happen to good people?" In an elementary sense, this question seems to settle it for many people. What they are really saying is, "If I were god, I would call this person and that person "good" and make sure bad things never happened to them."

More simply, such statements are tantamount to saying "The only god I'll worship is the god who does things the way I think everything ought to be done." Sound familiar? Of course, we have come far enough to realize that nobody is really good,[7] and even the best of us sinners still lives in a thoroughly corrupted world. Bad things will happen to everybody. Those things will happen without regard to who deserves them and people will suffer without deference to justice. "Bad things" are inevitably characteristic of living in a tragically broken, corrupted world in which every citizen has earned a broken relationship with the One who is qualified to restore perfection.

There is another question which is less frequently asked. "Why do good things so often come out of bad circumstances?" Why do tragedies pull people together? Why does jointly suffering with another human tend to forge strong bonds with that person? Why do many struggles make us stronger? Why does poverty inspire compassion? Why do we long for God when we are most afraid? How can wisdom be found in the midst of realizing consequences? If there was no God or if He were very distant, our concepts of bad actions would result in bad things and good would be good. If there was no God, bad would not ever result in good. Yet, even in this world, full of corruption as it is, "good" is still very evident. Sometimes it is most evident in the darkest of times. This good is not a result of ourselves, but it persists because God is real and active among us.

This world in which "bad things" happen is a world that is constantly suffering the consequences of evil. By natural consequences, sin is "punished" both on an individual basis and across humankind.[8] We can be sure that a just God will, in the eternal scope, make certain that justice is distributed for better or for worse, though we will not likely see full justice as long as we live in such a broken world.[9]

Natural Consequences and the Devil's Role: Section Summary

- *The world in which we live is rife with the consequences of sin. The corruption of the world is the reason why "bad things" and "good things" do not seem to proportionately reward and punish behaviors according to natural consequences.*

- *A world in which each individual has tried to become his or her own god is a world that has sided with the Devil in enmity with the true God.*

- *The decision to worship the Devil is the default result of choosing not to worship God. The Devil wants you to seal your doom by turning you from God.*

- *The Devil hates you and is bent on your destruction. As the father of lies, he does not immediately care what you believe so long as it is not true.*

DEBT VS. PUNISHMENT

In the previous section we discussed natural consequences and punishment for evil. Our bigger concern than punishment should be our concern with debt. Involuntary debt (as opposed to debt from a voluntary loan) is not necessarily a punishment; it is a mechanism for reconciling loss or destruction within the standards of perfect justice. Debt, unlike a "fine", is the amount required to restore some broken or destroyed thing to a state of wholeness. A parking ticket may result in a "fine" as punishment, but we are referring to true, involuntary "debt", not a fine. A parking ticket fine does not restore the space to having been empty when the meter ran out, nor is it based on the amount of revenue that meter could have generated while the car was illegally parked. Debt is a function of restoration. It is of much larger significance. Perfect repayment of debt is able to make something injured by wrong as good as or even better than it originally was.

Punishment is for the benefit of the offender: it teaches, instructs, and modifies behavior.[1] Debt, when perfectly repaid, is for the benefit of both the offended and the offender. It restores the offender to good standing and restores the offended to wholeness. When we sin, we offend God's righteousness.

Consequences of sin are something that we can theoretically deal with on a human basis, even though those consequences drive every single one of us to an early grave. What we are not able to effectively solve is our debt to righteousness. Adam and Eve received mandated consequences for their actions. Much worse, however, was that they were justifiably removed from God's presence with no hope of somehow working their way back in. They went from living in perfect Eden to living in a world under the curse of sin where they would live to see their children murder each other.

In terms of righteousness, our overwhelming debt problem is that we have no capacity to restore ourselves to wholeness with God. We cannot re-make ourselves perfect. If we have any hope whatsoever of being righteously restored to perfection in order to live forever with our Creator, it will have to come from outside of ourselves.

Debt vs. Punishment: Section Summary

- *Punishment is for the benefit of the offender: it teaches, instructs, and modifies behavior. Debt is for the benefit of both the offended and the offender. It restores the offender to good standing and restores the offended to wholeness or restore ourselves to righteousness.*

- *We have offended God's righteousness with our sin. Our debt continues to exist because we do not have the means in and of ourselves to restore righteousness to wholeness.*

- *Any hope of restoration to our Creator must come from something beyond us.*

THE COST OF RECONCILIATION

Remember our example when I was facing such heavy punishment for the crimes I committed when I totaled your priceless car? I had no chance of bearing up under a sentence delivered by a just judge. I was on the wrong end of the law. I could not pay my debt. As a result, the court's justice would crush me without being able to fix the damage to your car or heal the injured bus passengers. I would lose my freedom and be cut off from society. Because of my lawlessness, I could not bear up under the weight of justice as demanded by righteousness. In the same way, our sin has brought upon us a penalty we cannot abide. Because we are unable to restore our own perfection, we must be cut off from God. To be cut off from God forever is the definition of Hell. Unless there is another solution, the penalty is our eternal destruction as well as our Creator's eternal grief.

In our story about my crashing your car into the bus, the crime is large and the debt is overwhelming to the criminal but it is hardly an infinite crime. Beyond that example, our harsh reality is that we are guilty of sin, which infinitely disqualifies us from being accepted by God. Our corrupted nature defies His perfect nature and He cannot violate His own laws because they are an extension of His infinite nature. Accordingly, our real problem in this life is of infinite proportions. We cannot pay the debt even for our most mundane sins because we, soiled as we are, are all wrong for the payment of sin. Could a righteous God be satisfied with an unrighteous payment?[1] Would a just judge knowingly accept dirty money as payment for a crime? All of our efforts are tainted. Because we are sinful, we cannot produce righteous payment. In the ancient laws which once allowed us to approach God on a limited basis, the spilling of perfect blood according to righteous standards represented a payment for sin. You and I, however, have no perfect blood to offer.

Logically, we know that payment of an infinite debt would command an infinite price. We also know that we simply do not have the capacity to pay an infinite price. In the entire universe, there is only One Being with infinite capacity and that is God Himself. The God of the Universe, our own Creator, the very Judge of our crimes, is the only sacrifice so perfect that it could qualify as a total payment for any amount of sin.

The very idea that a righteous judge would give himself for the payment of somebody else's debts is nothing short of absurd. Upright judges are dignified and criminals are not. Judges wear flowing robes and sit at the highest point of the courtroom. Judges have fancy hammers whose poundings signal that justice has been served. Judges have no business mixing with criminals, common or otherwise.

How much more so Almighty God and soiled humanity! By human standards, He has no business trying to pay for the problems we enthusiastically brought on ourselves. Even if He wanted to, how can God accept a punishing debt on behalf of humanity? He is a spirit and we are flesh. He cannot be sacrificed because, as an immortal spirit, He cannot die. Remember, true death is to be separated from God who is the source of all life. How could God be separated from Himself? And who would do the punishing? Would He extract payment from Himself? Banish the thought! We have real problems here that need real solutions. We desperately need an actual, workable solution before… before Hell breaks loose on all humanity.

But there is no other solution.

Is that it, then? If our relationship with God is already broken, if our debt to a righteous law is too high for us to pay and we are unable to do anything about it, are we not all doomed to Hell anyway? Are we wasting our time to even bother looking for a way out?

If God does not rescue us from ourselves and supply some way of reconciling our relationship with Him without violating justice then we are all damned… and justly so.

If God knows everything, surely He knew this would happen. If He knew we would be doomed, why would He even have created us? I did not volunteer to be part of some sick joke. Sure, I played a voluntary role in sinning, but I could hardly help myself and now we are talking about eternal damnation here.

Would a loving God abandon us to such a horrible fate?

He would not. He is loving and He has not abandoned us to a horrible fate.

Because He is a perfect father who loves his children no matter how foolish they are, our peril compels our heavenly father to action. God does not hold Himself to a merely human concept of justice. He will offer us a way out even if He has to give every ounce of Himself - which is exactly how much of Him is required.

It is true that there are obstacles to be overcome before justice can be served. We are flesh and God is spirit, but He created flesh. What would stop Him from choosing to assume flesh and live life in a fragile, error-prone earthly body like our own?[2] Humiliating, yes - in human terms - especially for the mightiest, most righteous being in all existence. Humiliating, but not impossible. A human being would be inhibited by protecting his own pride. For the God of the Universe, pride is unnecessary and therefore cannot be injured. The human concept of humiliation is not the barrier to Him that it is to you or me.

In order to pay a debt owed by humanity God would have to assume full humanity, thereby exposing Himself to everything that is the human plight: cold, loneliness, sadness, frustration, pain, grief, dismay, betrayal, rejection, exhaustion, injustice, poverty, hunger, sorrow, and suffering would all become intimate and familiar experiences if God was to become human. It may not sound impressive considering that practically every person who has ever lived has swallowed at least a hint of those bitter pills. But we humans are subject to sin. We are our own problem. If God was to become human, He would be facing something He utterly did not deserve… and He would have to face it perfectly. If, in the absolute peril of assuming human weakness, Almighty God fell to sin even once, as you and I do every day, He would be as subject to righteous wrath as we ourselves. In other words, unless God was an absolutely perfect human according to the standard of righteousness, there would be no rescue from sin and the entire universe would be given over to utter corruption.

Step with me for a moment into the role of a hypothetical, external spectator to the cosmic scene unfolding so far. Pretend, you and I, that we are observing the totality of God's actions toward humanity from afar, with a non-human perspective, maybe as some intelligent fly on the wall in heaven. Maybe we witnessed the jaw-dropping creation of the universe and we gasped and cheered as He brought forth all of creation in its Eden-era perfection.[3] The stars, the majestic earth itself, then the plants, the birds and fish in all their varieties, and then, in a special process, this curious new creation, mankind, with humans called "man" and "woman". "*Quite a nice display*" we might say to ourselves. And then we would learn that this "Heavens and earth" was not just an object lesson in principles of creativity, but that God had made mankind in His own image and was granting those humans free wills of their own. Not only were they getting free will, but every human ever conceived would be given an eternal soul of its own. Surely heaven was full of gasps and whispers of admiration and awe at the very concept as the gravity of what God had created sunk in and the news spread between the angels. "*Did you hear? Humans are to be eternal,*[4] *and free to choose between good or evil!*[5] *What if they choose evil and corrupt that beautiful world God just created? At least those humans are not very powerful.*[6] *Who could forget when Lucifer, one of the most powerful among us, tried to become like God and instead became the*

Devil? What a war that was! Wait… is that him in the beautiful garden of Eden? Why, he's talking to Eve! Oh, Eve, don't listen to him! He's a liar! You can't be your own god!" And then the fall, the shock and sadness as wickedness spread like an epidemic throughout the world. The suffering, the pain, and death! Oh so much death. How awful to watch souls wrenched from the bodies and then, those once lovely bodies, originally planned and personally crafted by God's own fingers, now subjected to grisly decay. Surely the angels turned their eyes away and wept for the great sadness of it all. But none of them felt it as deeply as God Himself. To Him, every act of wickedness was the pain of unrequited love. Every bit of cruelty was one of His long-lost, beloved children inflicting it on another. He did not sit idly by. He sent prophets, set up guidelines, enabled miracles, personally manifested Himself to entire nations, spoke with wise men, had it all written down, preserved, and widely distributed. He publicly punished some of the worst sins and established natural consequences to reward those who tried to please Him, but it was clear that every single human had been marred by sin.[7] One by one, their bodies would succumb to the brokenness of the world and the souls, now freed from flesh but guilty of all kinds of sin, would have to be banished from God's presence. What a tragic waste! The heavenly beings must have been numb with shock as it became clear that

God's beloved creation - beautiful, naïve, and foolish - had fallen entirely into the hands of Lucifer, the Devil. Had God lost this battle? Unthinkable! But what could He do? Sin is sin and nobody but God Himself could cover the debt of this much sin against His own righteous law.

But then... Oh! What news! God was going to pay the debt Himself. How would the heavenly beings have responded? *"Is that possible? Is that even legal? Wouldn't He have to actually be human to pay human debt? But He created them and they ruined everything He ever made! You're telling me He's going to become one of them! No human, not even the best of them, has ever managed to exercise his own free will without regularly sinning against God. How can God become human?"*

God would personally save humanity from itself. He would become fully human, including free will and an eternal spirit: He would live a human life. He would subject Himself to the very worst of humanity. He would face every human temptation. He would be meek and would actually serve other humans while He lived on earth. He would, without sinning, assume personal responsibility for all sin ever committed. He would submit himself to the righteous wrath required against sin... all of it. He would be cut off from the land of the living. He would consequently die, broken, rejected, and utterly alone. He would do all of this perfectly. He would do all of this voluntarily and obediently. If it worked, human beings would have at least a chance of avoiding Hell, assuming they still wanted to.

Do you get a sense of the utter unbelievability of God's plan to save humanity? Even the very heavenly beings must have been astonished, awed, and maybe even a little confused as they wondered how it would play out.[8] After all, it is no accident that "human" includes the root word "hum" which means "earth" or "dirt". To be humble is to be "down to earth", perhaps even dirty. To be human is to be earthly. For the God of Heaven to become a man on earth would be, in every sense, both the humiliation and the triumph of God.

The Cost of Reconciliation: Section Summary

- *Unless our debt to righteousness, the wages of sin, is paid then we are doomed.*

- *Only God has the capacity to pay the unfathomable cost of satisfying His own righteous law and restoring us to perfect standing with Him, thus saving us from Hell.*

- *God loves us so much that He was willing to rescue us from the condemnation brought upon us by our sin, even at a tremendous cost to Himself.*

- *In order to satisfy justice, the full payment of humanity's debt of sin would have to be extracted from humanity itself.*

- *God would save humanity by becoming perfectly yet completely human and accepting the entirety of His own law's charge against humanity on His own, human self.*

TERMS OF REDEMPTION

Paying a price to move somebody from being condemned to being in good standing by paying the condemned one's debt in his place is called "redemption".[1] Redemption is a transaction. We have spent much time discussing the context, the need, and the requirements of the repurchase of humanity by God from the clutches of sin. Let us review the answers to the critical questions around this transaction:

What must be purchased?

The Redeemer is purchasing the legally justified possibility of your personal relationship with your Creator. If sin is not fully dealt with, we have to bear the eternal consequences of being sinners. By taking sin on Himself and dealing with it there, God purchases the legal right to let us re-choose Him[2] as our God and quit trying to be our own gods. Only then, when we turn to Him as God, can He re-engage us in full relationship and begin rebuilding our hearts.

By whom?

Only God Himself can pay the infinite price required to count you, who are imperfect, to be qualified for His perfect presence. You and I have a debt to His law and that debt must be paid in order for us to be counted as righteous under that law.

From whom?
You and I are being redeemed from the just consequences demanded by a perfectly righteous system of law, which is enforced by God Himself. We are not being bought back from Satan on Satan's terms, though we fell prey to the same lie that sealed his doom ("You can be like God"). The law that damns us is a reflection of God's perfect character, as is His selflessness that saves us.[3] Incredibly, we are saved according to the same righteousness that would otherwise condemn us.

At what cost?
Our redemption will cost God everything to which He is entitled.[4] While He would be justified in distancing Himself from us forever, He instead chooses to become one of us for our benefit. He volunteers to face personal rejection and humiliation at the hands of the very loved ones He is trying to save.

Reconciliation with God also requires something of us, but it is a very different cost: like a drowning man letting go of a boulder at the bottom of a river, we must let go of self-worship. How can we be reconciled to the true God if we continue to try and replace Him with our unworthy selves? How can we be in relationship with a God we refuse to rightfully acknowledge?

Why does it matter?

If God does not save us from our own decision to turn from Him, we are eternally doomed to separation from Him, which is Hell. By giving us the chance to re-enter perfect relationship with Him, we can be rescued from the tyranny of trying to be our own gods. If we embrace God as the one, true God by fully turning from our sinful ways, if we acknowledge Him as our savior from sin and from ourselves, we can be fully restored to the benefits of being children of a heavenly Father. These benefits are most wholly manifested in eternity with God, after we are done with our mortal, sin-submitted bodies on earth.

How is our Redemption Transacted?

The redemption of humankind from our debt to sin is birthed, lived out, executed, and proved in the person of Jesus Christ.[5]

JESUS CHRIST

Jesus Christ is the physical person of God in genuine human form.[1] Jesus is fully God as well as fully human. His God-hood is not constrained by His being a human, nor is His human-ness constrained by His being God. Only God Himself could save us from the wrathful judgment which was legally required to be poured out against humankind. A mere representative of God, no matter how closely resembling the true God, would not have been enough. It had to be God Himself. Similarly, a non-human could not have been a satisfactory human payment for a human debt. Jesus is the only being who could fit the bill on both accounts: He is completely, entirely, human and He is completely, entirely, God. Because His love for His beloved creation has no bounds, God Almighty willingly joined His own creation in order to fully pay the debt owed by humanity. Jesus Christ bent His knee to righteousness[2] and accepted punishment that otherwise would have been yours and mine. He paid the debts that you and I could never have paid.

Remember how we can manifest ourselves differently for different purposes? We discussed the example of how a woman can be a friend, a wife, a mother, and a daughter without compromising her singular self. Similarly, but even more so, God is Himself in at least three distinct ways: the Father, the Son, and the Holy Spirit. These three distinct beings of God are sometimes referred to as "the Trinity". Jesus Christ is "the Son". He took earthly human form for our benefit. He is as fully God as the Father or the Holy Spirit, but He exists as a distinct human person while still being God.[3] Jesus, being a human, is not distinct from God, but rather He is distinct as God.

Without compromising His own Godhood, God as Jesus Christ submitted Himself to His own law. In a sense, Jesus is not so much God's representative to humanity as He is humanity's representative to God. Because we are so woefully unable to effectively represent ourselves in the light of God's perfection, God provided a perfect, human representative for us - Himself in human form. He willingly chose to forego His majesty, His glory, the heavenly adulation that was due Him, His position, His beauty, His being worshipped, and the benefits and rank to which He was legitimately entitled.

More mysteriously, God was willing to be veiled from perfect communion with His own Self. He became "Son" while "Father" remained in Heaven. As "Son", Jesus Christ became obedient to God the Father, whom He sought to please in all things. Though He is

God, Jesus lived as the picture of a true servant. Even as God in human form, Jesus Christ did not assert Himself or His human will. Instead, contrary to every other human being who has ever lived, Jesus only embraced the will of the Father. In spite of facing every temptation common to humankind, He never once deviated from the Father's will.[4] As a result, Jesus is rightfully counted as perfect and sinless. Jesus worked out God's righteous law perfectly both in heart and in action.

Besides being perfect in action, Jesus is perfect in love. His presence on earth is only explained by His love for us. Without love, there is no other reason why God should undergo humiliation and willingly suffer for the sake of a bunch of human beings who willfully rejected Him before He even arrived. Indeed, Jesus Christ openly demonstrated servanthood on many levels specifically so that we could understand the depth of His love for us.[5]

How would you expect this world of ours to react to a person who was a living definition of righteousness as well as the very embodiment of selfless love? Would you expect that all of humanity would naturally flock to the person of Jesus, would see that God's will is better than our own will, would recognize His perfection and would forsake our sinful ways in order to please Him? Would we acknowledge His example as the answer to our problems? Would our fallen and corrupted world embrace this man and submit our hearts to Him?

Or, would we instead be fascinated in an alien way by this human who was so like us but so not like us? Would we try to use Him for our own material benefit? Would we become frustrated with Him and desert Him when we could not fully grasp the mysteries He showed us? Would we become distinctly uncomfortable with His poignant words? Would we try to play Him into our own politics? Would we shout insults at Him? Would we accuse Him and try to trap Him? Would we betray Him and leave Him alone in His darkest hour? Would we deny even knowing Him in front of His accusers? Would we accuse Him of being from the Devil, condemn Him to death, mock Him and spit in His face? Would we literally do our worst to Him and either stand by or actively participate while He was publicly, humiliatingly murdered in cold blood?

What if Jesus Christ quietly moved into your house? How would you react to Him? What if He joined you, uninvited, in your every waking moment?

When God manifested in human flesh and joined humankind on earth, He did not bring His kingly attributes with Him. Rather, He was poor, ordinary, of low rank, and lived much of

His life quietly.[6] He arrived with no estate and died with no possessions. He brought only good and benefit for His fellow humanity. As peripheral parts of His redeeming work, He healed the sick, encouraged the lowly, advocated for right treatment of one another, protected the oppressed, challenged the oppressors, raised the dead, taught the truth, and backed up everything He did with undisputable miracles.[7] Yet, He was hated. Before his death, very few who had encountered Jesus had more than a fragmented understanding of who He was, despite Christ's clear assertions and proofs of His own deity.[8] His clarity was confusing to our corrupted minds. He was revered by some for a time, but it was largely out of selfish ambition and the hope that Jesus would seize political power. Jesus did not come from Heaven in order to seize human power.[9] As a result, when push came to shove then everybody deserted Him and kept their distance.[10] Jesus was barely beginning his public ministry when some people were already plotting against His life.[11] In the end, it was only a matter of time before He was murdered with the public fully aware and largely approving of the execution.[12]

If humankind was already in a position to welcome a righteous God with open arms then we might not have needed a savior in the first place. In our corrupted state, we have a fundamental incompatibility with God. As a result, when God incarnate joined us in the person of Jesus Christ, He did not find like minds and like hearts. He did not bring a great sense of unity and royally usher in Heaven on earth.[13] Rather, He expected to be despised, rejected, and murdered. God even sent prophets well in advance of Jesus' arrival who would describe in vivid detail how Jesus, the savior of humankind, would be hated by those He came to save.

If, in the wake of His death, you are wondering what the point of Jesus' life on earth really was, you have that in common with His disciples immediately after Jesus' crucifixion. Although He gave the explicit warning that He was primarily on earth to be killed as a divine sacrifice,[14] Jesus' disciples were initially confused and dismayed by His death. They did not understand that, in becoming the willing and perfect sacrifice,[15] Jesus had made full payment of our debt.[16]

Because He alone fulfilled the requirements for a perfect payment of debt, Jesus Christ became the only way a sinful person can possibly be restored to God.[17] We are restored to God by participating in Christ, which requires us to renounce being our own gods, turn from our sin,[18] and believe in Christ and what He did for us.[19] God takes this "death to ourselves" on the credit of the full payment that Jesus Christ provided on the cross.[20] The result is that we, imperfect as we are, can be counted as though we are perfect.[21]

Bear in mind that participating in Christ is much more than simply believing that He exists or existed. Participating in Christ means voluntarily foregoing ownership of our own selves - just as Jesus did when He chose to live on earth as a humble servant - and turning to Christ as Lord of our very existence. If we want to be with God, we must let go of the lie that we somehow have ownership of ourselves. That self-ownership has placed us under slavery to sin.[22] We never really owned ourselves anyway. We have been perhaps unaware but nevertheless active participants in the Devil's domain ever since we tried to be our own gods. In paying our debt to righteousness for us, Jesus bought us the option to choose to be under His ownership rather than the Devil's ownership. He is offering us the chance of being redeemed from slavery to sin and death.[23] He enables the choice to submit ourselves to righteousness and to God's perfect law, which Jesus Christ brought to fulfillment.[24] Otherwise, we choose corruption and an ill-fitting eternity of misery and frustration. We were originally created to be with God. We can be sure that choosing to be with God is the perfect choice. Jesus' perfect death paid for the legal right to justly accept us when we make the decision to reject the old corruption, turn from the delusion of self-rule, and humbly ask for God to forgive us and bring us back to Him.

If we approach God by Christ, we are counted as qualified to be welcomed by our heavenly Father and embraced as His long-lost children.[25] If we approach God on our own merit or on the merit of any besides Christ, we have nothing to show which would perfectly qualify us to be embraced by a perfect God.[26] God's only righteous option is to reject us, to His own grief, unless we approach Him under the payment accomplished by Christ.[27]

Because Christ accomplished all that was necessary, there is no need for any other savior. God has not made himself known to humankind in any other human form besides Jesus Christ, and He has not willingly offered himself as a perfect sacrifice for all of humanity under any other name besides that of Jesus Christ.[28]

Jesus Christ: Section Summary

- *Jesus Christ is the physical person of God in human form. He is fully human and fully God. In order to pay our debt to righteousness in our place, God willingly became fully human. As the person of Jesus Christ, God died in our place, as a human, for our benefit, and met a standard of perfection utterly beyond our ability. He paid our debt in full!*

- *Jesus lived a perfect human life and was completely sinless. His will was perfectly aligned with the Heavenly Father's will. When we perceive Him from a sinful, human perspective, Jesus' perfection both fascinates us and challenges our inherent corruption. As a result, He was murdered in an act of complete rebellion against God and was thus subjected to all the fury of sin and death.*

- *Jesus is the embodiment of God's love for us. At great personal cost to Himself, God offers Himself, as Jesus Christ, to be the singular and perfect instrument of humanity's salvation.*

- *Christ's perfection can cover an infinite amount of our imperfection. To be counted under Christ, to participate in Christ, is much more than simply believing He exists. We must turn to Him as Lord and God.*

- *If we approach God by Christ's perfect merit instead of our own insufficiencies, we can be accepted as though we are completely worthy to be with God.*

A CAUTION

Any attempt to describe the exact nature of our salvation from sin must take for granted a particular risk of failing to accurately capture the full scope of God's intervention. God is mysterious. God appearing in human form and willfully dying in order to restore broken humanity to being counted as perfect under God's own law of righteousness is downright mind-boggling.[1] In other words, without compromising accuracy, we cannot make something simple which is inherently beyond our earthly comprehension. If you find yourself getting too caught up in trying to pin down the exact mechanism of salvation, you run the risk of missing the whole point of Christ. Christ is the only way to God,[2] which is all we really must grasp. To be restored to good standing with our Creator, we are required to believe in Christ, including the person, identity, action, result, and nature of Christ, and to accept our need for Him. Though we must know Him, we are not necessarily required to fully understand Christ, thank goodness.[3] We are not even required to be able to thoroughly articulate our rudimentary understanding of Christ, though it is good to try. "Jesus Christ is Lord" is a good place to start.[4]

Although God has graciously given us thinking minds, it would be a mistake to rely too heavily on our own understanding, especially of mysteries which have not yet been fully revealed to us.[5] We can accept God's word because He said it and He revealed the message to us, not because we somehow arrived at the same conclusion in our own reasoning. If we insist on working it all out in our own minds, we are ultimately attempting to replace God's truth with our own intellects.

So far, we have discussed our redemption from sin in the framework of a transaction.[6] You can be sure that our understanding of transactions is not enough to enable us to completely grasp cosmic mysteries.[7] We participate in forming transactions practically every day, yet even mundane earthly transactions have some mystery around them. For example, what exactly is "ownership" and how does it shift between individuals? What is the exact mechanism that triggers rightful ownership to change from "yours" to "mine"? Transactions are mysterious. There are other frameworks which can be helpful in describing the necessity of Christ and the power of His death for us. However, no framework or combination of explanations can possibly give a full, accurate, and perfect explanation of precisely how - or even why - God restores us to Himself. Rather, the important thing is to accept that we need to be restored to God, that we cannot do so on our own merit, and that God's perfect intervention for our benefit is Himself as Jesus Christ. From those truths, God actively cultivates greater understanding in our hearts.

Once we have believed in Him, our goal is to know Jesus by building a relationship with Him. Knowing about Him is peripheral to the real purpose of actually knowing Him. If we spent every day of the rest of our lives deliberately building our individual relationships with Jesus Christ, we would not miss any good thing.

A Caution: Section Summary

- *There is an inherently mysterious element to the salvation transaction. At some point, we must be willing to take a leap: we must shift from relying exclusively on our inadequate understanding of this cosmic mystery and accept that God has revealed Christ to us so that we can believe in Him and acknowledge our need for Him.*

- *God has given us good minds, but with limits. We should apply our minds to knowing and loving Him. In the end, what matters is belief, meaning faith, in the person of Jesus Christ to save us from our sin. We are not required to fully understand the unfathomable depths of what God has really done for us. Our focus should be the person of Christ; we should pursue knowing Him, not merely knowing about Him.*

PROOF

If we are to rely so heavily on Christ and His death for us, we will reasonably look for evidence that our debt is actually paid in full. In other words, how do we know that it worked? How can we be sure that the divine transaction actually bought us back from sin and certain death?

First, Christ Himself is a picture of humanity bearing the burden of sin and then being restored to everlasting life with the Father in Heaven. He demonstrated the full process for us.

Put more bluntly, we know it worked because Jesus did not stay dead. He rose to everlasting life with the Father. His resurrection from death under the penalty of sin and His restoration to eternal life proves that He successfully became the way to God.[1]

Jesus had died a public death. He had been thoroughly, verifiably dead after being crucified.[2] If Jesus Christ had stayed dead, it would call into question a very important claim, namely that God is the source of life and that death is a function of being separated from God.[3] Jesus took the sin of the world on Himself. Though the sins were not originally

His own, He was rightly separated from God while He was bearing the sin of all humanity. When Jesus died as perfect and total payment for that sin, the power of sin to result inevitably in death was shattered. If Jesus had remained dead, it would have been evidence that the sin-death curse was not fully broken because the restoration of life would first have been applied to the One who paid for it.[4] More ominously, if Jesus had stayed dead in the tomb it would have been God Himself being overwhelmed and vanquished by death. If Christ's resurrection had never happened, what confidence could you and I have that we are not still under the same curse?

We can be thankful that Jesus not only rose from the dead, He did it in an unmistakable manner. After His resurrection from the dead, He spent many days walking the earth and met in person with hundreds of people, many of whom had personally witnessed His death.[5] This public resurrection was a crucial factor in the early rise of the first followers of Christ. Think about it: the same people who had deserted Jesus when He was arrested were now willing to put their reputations, their livelihoods, and their very lives on the line while publicly claiming that Jesus was, in fact, alive. Nobody tried to claim that Jesus had not died. Everybody knew He had died. Yet, here were hundreds and soon to be thousands of otherwise normal people insisting that Jesus was alive and healthy.

Within mere days of Christ's public execution, powerful religious leaders who hated Christ were scrambling to stamp out the claims that Jesus had not stayed dead.[6] Those leaders understood that a risen Jesus was indisputable proof of Jesus' claims about who He really was. If Jesus' body was still in that tomb, why did they not simply open up the tomb, put the dead body on display (like they had displayed the death) and crush the silly rumors that Jesus was alive and walking around? They did not do so because they could not. The body was not available. It was not in the tomb even though those religious leaders had taken drastic measures to be sure the tomb was secure.[7] In spite of their authority and credibility being on the line, the leaders made no effort to find the body because even they knew they never would. Where they needed proof of lasting death, they instead had proof of everlasting life. Jesus had risen, just as He said He would. If He had not risen, it should have been easy to prove that He was dead… except the proof of death had gotten up and walked away. This resurrection was so convincing that it was only a matter of time before thousands of early Christ-followers went to their own grisly deaths[8] still insisting that Jesus was alive.

Proof: Section Summary

- *Jesus' rising from the dead is proof that the power of death over sin-burdened humanity has been broken. The transaction worked! By rising from the dead, Jesus proved that sin no longer has to result in death.*

- *Jesus' resurrection was public and obvious. Hundreds of people who had witnessed Jesus' execution now were utterly convinced that He had risen from the dead. This public knowledge called the rulers' power into question, but they were at a loss to explain Jesus' walking out of His tomb after three days of being dead.*

- *We can take comfort in the resurrection because it proves that Jesus really did conquer eternal death on our behalf. Because of Christ, sin no longer holds absolute condemnation over us!*

HOLY SPIRIT

We have a second proof that Jesus had broken down the major barrier between sinful humanity and a righteous God. Since Christ's death, God has engaged men and women on a spirit level. In other words, starting in the days immediately after Jesus' return to Heaven, God's Holy Spirit was openly manifesting Himself[1] in those who had come to believe that Jesus was God. Such communion between God's Spirit and human spirits was not possible in the absence of Christ's death and resurrection.

Do not be confused by this concept of spirit-to-spirit engagement. In movies or books we might see dramatic scenes of spirits taking over bodies of mortals or causing all sorts of havoc in a séance. On the contrary, when the Holy Spirit of the living God influences your spirit or my spirit, it is a reflection of that perfect relationship with God for which we were created.[2] In addition to being flesh as Jesus Christ, God is spirit. The spirit manifestation of God is referred to as the Holy Spirit. Remember the Trinity? The Holy Spirit is the third distinct manifestation of God after the Father and the Son.[3] It makes sense that He would engage with us through the individual spirits that He gave to us when He created us.

Our spirit is where God is able to gain an intensely personal foothold in our being. It is through the Holy Spirit that God can start His work of healing the wounds of living in a corrupted world. If we accept Jesus Christ as our Lord, the Holy Spirit gives us new life and starts a transformative work in us that continues for the rest of our lives.[4] God is the great healer. Though we cannot change our own hearts, He can change our hearts for us. Even after believing in Christ, we can choose, tragically, to push Him away and resist His ongoing work. We do better if we choose to quit flailing about and let His Spirit gently restore our hearts, hour by hour, for the rest of our lives on earth.

The purposes of God's Holy Spirit include guiding, counseling, instructing, enlightening, strengthening, encouraging, and empowering those who, by Jesus Christ, are no longer cut off from God by an insurmountable debt to perfection.[5] As long as we are on earth, we struggle against our own corruption and will never be made perfect. With God's Spirit alive and active in us, we do not have to struggle ineffectively or on our own power.[6] You can be sure that living in a corrupted world is much easier with the active presence of the Holy Spirit in our hearts than if we were to face the world all alone.[7]

What if God's Holy Spirit did not engage with us? A person is reconciled to God through

Christ voluntarily. In choosing to stop serving oneself as god and to begin serving the true God, a corrupted human being faces a problem: even when we try hard, on our own power we are very bad at doing what God wants while being consistently good at doing what He does not want us to do. Because we had broken away from God and become ungodly, we would make awkward friends of God even if we were willing. Our hearts are inherently selfish and corrupted. We have to become changed people to live out what God asks of us. If God did not actively engage us and do healing work in our spirits and hearts, our relationship with Him would be very strained indeed. We can be thankful that God is there to help us and equip us to know and understand Him better every day that we are willing to listen.

We can see proof that Jesus Christ effectively paid our debt and allowed us to be justifiably restored to our Creator when we see the evidence of the Holy Spirit in individuals who have given themselves to God by Christ.[8]

The early disciples are a good example of this change. Shortly before His death, Jesus explained His purpose, His identity, His impending death, and even the Holy Spirit in clear terms to His closest disciples. However, because they were trying to understand it all with their own human intellects, they were confused. They even argued between themselves as they tried to sort out what Jesus meant. They were afraid to tell Jesus they did not understand. On their own strength, they made grandiose statements about never deserting Jesus and even being willing to die for Him. Mere hours later, they deserted Him to a man. After His death, they went into hiding and sat around mourning and depressed. In other words, they had missed the whole point.

Look at the change in the disciples when the promised Holy Spirit began to work in their hearts! Those same confused, scared, bickering men suddenly began to understand all the things Jesus had been telling them for years. They lost all fear and began publicly explaining in detail the mysteries of God on earth as Jesus Christ.[9] In spite of persecution, they gave themselves over to truth. At the same time, through the disciples, God began revealing Himself to the very people who had murdered Him. Literally thousands of people suddenly began to understand and clearly see who Jesus really was. Many of them would suffer tremendous persecution and even death for their belief, but they accepted it joyfully. To prove His legitimacy to early skeptics, the Holy Spirit empowered otherwise ordinary men to perform miracles on the same scale that Jesus Himself had performed. This level of regeneration is more than just change. This is new birth.

The Holy Spirit had been active among humankind from time to time even before Jesus physically walked the earth. This previous activity was also possible because of the payment Jesus would make. Jesus would die once for all humankind, past, present, and future. However, it was not until after Jesus' death and resurrection that the Holy Spirit began to engage with otherwise ordinary people on a consistent basis.

In the same way that the disciples were changed by the Holy Spirit, you and I can be changed.[10] If we throw ourselves upon God's mercy rather than our own strength, if we give up our sin and stop trying to be our own gods, if we turn to our Heavenly Father and ask Him to accept us because we believe Jesus died for us as God so that we could be accepted, then, in that very moment,[11] our sin no longer stands between us and our Heavenly Father. By the blood of His Son, the Father will welcome us joyfully back to Himself and the Holy Spirit will begin a lifetime of His changing work in us.

Holy Spirit: Section Summary

- *The Holy Spirit's vibrant engagement with humanity is further proof that Jesus successfully overcame the sin barrier between humanity and God.*

OUR ROLE

In light of the proofs offered to us of Christ's effectiveness on the cross, what do we have to do to be counted as His? If the alternative is to face condemnation by our sin and expect eternal separation from our Heavenly Father, how do we take part in this salvation manifested by Christ? To be offered a rescue from well-earned condemnation is to be offered an undeserved gift of infinite value. We have thoroughly earned our status of ungodliness. We cannot un-earn our imperfection, which has eternal and tragic consequences. Because of His great love for us, and at an unfathomable personal cost to Himself, God has purchased a gift for us. He has purchased our salvation from our sin with all the benefits of being restored to our Creator forever. He offers this salvation to us freely.

What is our role in accepting this gift?

Like accepting any magnificent gift, your role is to simply accept the gift. It is no good trying to earn the gift. It is no good trying to rationalize that the gift was rightfully yours all along. To attempt to deserve the gift or to think you have a right to it not only scorns the generosity of the giver but also diminishes the value of the gift.

The thing about accepting a gift is that it cannot be done without some level of humility. You have to acknowledge that you need and want the gift. By nature, to accept a gift is to acknowledge that somebody else has the power to offer you something that you desire to possess yet have not earned. If it were earned, it would not be a gift but a wage or a payment. To accept a gift is to demonstrate a heart that says "I want what you are offering to me, I understand that it is rightfully yours and not mine, and I am grateful for this opportunity to obtain it." While, between us humans, we can fake that humility when we accept earthly gifts, it is impossible to fool God with false humility.

Just as accepting a gift demonstrates something about the heart of the one receiving it, the offering of a gift demonstrates even more about the giver. There is no single term which fully captures all that Jesus Christ did on the cross. He not only paid our debt, He also revealed much about the heart God has for us. Jesus did not personally take credit for dying for mankind. He consistently stated that He was sent by His Father in Heaven. What does Jesus Christ's willing death (not to mention His humble arrival on earth in the first place) show us about God the Father? If you spent a lifetime probing good answers for that question it would be a life well spent. For example, Jesus Christ showed us the Father's mercy. To be on the receiving end of mercy is an extraordinary thing. To receive mercy is to receive something which you very badly need but have no right to justly receive. Mercy is not something you can seize because it must be willingly given to you. If you know you desperately need mercy and it is willingly offered to you, what is the right response? The heart which best receives mercy is a heart that is humbled, inspired, overjoyed, grateful, penitent, and full of love for the one who extended such mercy. There are people who ask for mercy but, in their hearts, are really looking for a way to skirt the consequences they deserve. This type of person wants to take advantage of somebody else's mercy and will ultimately behave in a way that rubs the mercy in the face of the one who offered it. The sort of person who seeks mercy only to avoid deserved consequences is not the sort of person who can understand and accept what Christ did on the cross. Sadly, the one who scorns mercy is too focused on wanting to live under his own mastery. As a result, he will not let himself be counted under the blood of Christ. His pride stands in the way of rightfully acknowledging God.

Besides willingly accepting a gift with a grateful heart, our free will allows us another option, one which is rightfully ours when we are offered a gift: we can refuse a gift. There are two reasons why we would refuse a gift.

First, maybe we do not want what is being offered. If we think the gift is of no lasting value to us, if we cannot be easily rid of it and possessing it is more trouble than it is worth, we are likely to refuse the gift. The other reason we would refuse a gift is because we refuse to be humbled by the person offering it. To accept a gift is also to accept the person offering the gift. We cannot very well accept a genuinely offered gift from somebody and then throw the person out. If we did, we would appear cruel and spoiled. If you really were upset at the person offering the gift, you would refuse it. In human terms, if you have been recently hurt by the person offering you the gift and you are still angry about it, or if you are predisposed to utterly rejecting that person, you are not likely to humble yourself by accepting their gift no matter how valuable it is. Maybe you would even be glad if their feelings were hurt by your refusal.

Just as the nature of a gift reflects the feelings of the one offering it to you, our acceptance or refusal of a gift directly reflects our feelings about the one offering it. We only accept highly personal gifts from those people to whom we personally want to be closer. For example, a wife might gigglingly accept a gift of flirtatious lingerie from her husband, but it is highly unlikely that she would accept the same gift from a lurking stranger in the airport. She understands that a gift of intimate nature should only come from somebody very close to her. She is rightfully appalled, mortified, and perhaps even scared when the same item is offered by a stranger. Between us humans, this dynamic makes sense. It also makes sense when we contemplate accepting the gift offered to us by God.

Consider the gift of Jesus Christ. Jesus is the embodiment of our being reconciled to our Creator. What does it reveal about God, our Heavenly Father that He would give His own Son to suffer and die for our benefit?[1] We had utterly rejected God. We were sinners. We represented everything that was not of Him. We had refused to let Him be our God. We were destined to be legally separated from Him for all of eternity. We had grieved Him in every way possible. We had forgotten who He is,[2] but He had not forgotten us for a moment. Yet, God loves us.[3] Even when we are at our worst, He is willing to give up everything to offer us a chance to be reconciled to Him. He is willing to take our shame, our filth, our pride, our sin, and put it all under His own account so that He can embrace us and wrap His arms around us. This gift of reconciliation with the result of eternal life with our Creator is in every way the most intensely personal, unfathomably valuable, intimately significant, and profoundly meaningful gift that could possibly be offered to us.

All we have to do is accept the gift of love, mercy, and forgiveness He is offering us. Because of the heart an acceptance requires, there is no possible way to half-heartedly accept that gift. You can accept it or reject it.

While it sounds as simple as putting our pride aside and accepting the gift embodied by Christ, we find that putting our pride aside is no small matter. Most self-respecting people can imagine a circumstance in which they would be willing to suffer or forego something desirable in order to keep their pride and self-respect intact. There is nothing wrong with a healthy sense of self-respect. God is not asking us to put aside our self-worth. Indeed, part of accepting the gift is to realize that He values us on an inconceivable scale. Rather, it is the unhealthy sense of self that we must release. In other words, we will not let God be our god until we quit trying to be our own gods. We cannot be grateful for His forgiveness until we acknowledge our need to be forgiven. We will never desire to be eternally with Him until we admit the awfulness of being separated from Him. We will not relax into his mercy until we come to terms with our inability to fix ourselves. We will not love Him until we believe that He first loved us.[4]

Our role is not to "do" anything. Our role is to believe.[5] True belief is active because it reflects a changed heart. Accepting the gift of Jesus Christ requires a return to truth from falsehood. In the Garden of Eden, Eve tragically traded her belief in God's love for belief in a lie that she should try to become like God. In doing so, she scorned God's will and embraced herself instead. It was not the physical action of chewing a particular fruit that resulted in a broken relationship with God. It was Eve's heart which led to the action. It was that turning of her free will from embracing truth into rejecting the true God and embracing a lie. Our role in being saved is not to stop doing certain actions or start doing some other action. On the contrary, instead of believing in our own actions we are to believe in the action God took on our behalf as Jesus Christ. When we believe in Jesus Christ instead of ourselves, we believe the Truth.

What is it to "believe in Christ?" This belief goes far beyond simply believing in the existence of God or the existence of Jesus Christ. Likewise, it is much more than simply believing facts about the person of Christ. Believing in Christ is focused on the person, the character, and the identity of Christ. This level of belief is impossible without forming a personal relationship with Him. A relationship-based belief results in our giving up ourselves and throwing ourselves fully at the feet of our Creator because we believe that Jesus has covered our disqualifications. You cannot come to Christ believing that you, in and of yourself, are good enough to be accepted on your own merits. A self-focused approach to Christ reflects a misunderstanding of Christ's purpose on earth. Rather, to believe in Christ is to reject your old self and to turn completely to God. In doing so, we acknowledge God in every aspect of our lives. When you believe in Christ, you realize the ugliness and shame of your old, self-worshiping ways. To believe in Christ is to place yourself at the mercy of God with the confidence that, because of Christ's sacrifice for you, you will be gladly accepted.[6] This acceptance does not happen because of what you have done for yourself but because of how much God has done for you even while you were still a sinner. Complete belief in Christ results in an utter transformation in our hearts. A heart transformation changes everything about us. Belief in Christ gives control of a person's life to God, restores that person to the truth, and marks the Holy Spirit's uninhibited work in that person's life. To believe in Christ is to establish Him as our only refuge. This type of belief in Christ is called "faith". Faith is not something you do, but it is something that grows in you because of what Jesus has done, because of who He is, and because of how you come to know Him as your relationship with Him grows.

To place your faith in Christ is not merely to shift from being self-centered to being Christ-centered in terms of your day-to-day activities. It is much more than an improvement of conscious focus. The person who has given himself or herself to Christ has become a new person, one whose very being is a function of Christ. The Christ-follower's dependence for existence is knitted to Christ Jesus. It is like a change in organic structure, a new spiritual DNA which cannot be undone. All you have, are, or will be is forever in Him, for Him, by Him, and through Him. Once you are in Christ, your ongoing struggle against sin and corruption is from an alien part of you. That fallen element of your old nature now feels very temporary, like you are wearing a dirty garment which will one day be cast off completely when Jesus hands you new garments of pure white. Until then, your earthly self chafes against your Christ-driven, renewed nature. Your old nature diminishes day by day because Christ's Holy Spirit increases in you as you mature in your relationship with your Creator.

To an outside observer, there is a clear difference between a person before and after that person believes in and accepts Jesus Christ as Lord. If somebody openly states they believe in Jesus Christ and accepts Him as Lord of their life, it should be evident in that person's speech behavior.[7] That person will not be perfect, but the influence of the Holy Spirit should become more and more evident. Every Christ-follower is a work in progress. It is easy to see what work still needs to be done, but the progress should also become evident over time. This progress in our lives does not happen because of our own efforts at self-improvement, but because of the Holy Spirit's ongoing involvement in our hearts. As long as we live on earth, we will still make mistakes, still stumble occasionally into old patterns, and still sin. However, because a Christ-follower is no longer his own god[8] and exists in Christ's power, he becomes a better and more able servant to the true God!

Just as it only took a moment for Eve to reject God, it only takes a moment for you or me to truly accept Him and return to truth. In that moment of truly accepting God, you are denying lies and wedding yourself to the truth of Jesus Christ, including all that He is, all that He did, all that He represents, and all that He asks of you In that moment you give up being your own god, turn from your sin, and return to your rightful place as a child of the one, true God.

Because He already paid the full price for reconciliation, God does not need us to perfectly accept His gift in order for it to be fully, permanently, ours. He only needs that moment of truth in order to count us as perfect under the blood of Christ. When, by Christ, we are counted as perfect, all of our sins, past, present, and future, sins of action, sins of thought, sins of heart, sins of ignorance, and willful sins, they are all legally removed from our accounts.[9] As a result, our salvation from our sin is permanent and cannot be revoked. Just as we did not work to earn salvation for ourselves, we also do not un-earn salvation by our own works. Our belief in Christ is not the cause of our salvation; belief is the condition our hearts must be in so that Christ, who is the cause of our salvation, can be applied to our account. In other words, once we believe and accept the gift of Christ, we are saved![10]

Being saved from self-worship can occur in an instant. Restoration from corruption occurs over time. To be set apart from corruption is to become holy. Holiness is not about being better than somebody else. Indeed, such inclinations are what lead to corruption in the first place. Rather, to be holy is to have your purpose aligned with God's purpose for you. God's purpose for you is perfect not only for Him but also for you because He made you, He knows you, He loves you in spite of your shortcomings, and He has paid a very high price so that you no longer have to be the victim of those shortcomings you once chose.

How beautiful it is to live free from the sin that once enslaved you! No longer do you have to carry the weight of your fabricated self-worship. Reconciliation to your Creator includes reconciliation to the purposes for which you were created.[11] As a result, you can live with purpose, meaning, and no fear of the future. You can live in Christ! As long as you live in a broken and corrupted world you will still feel the effects of sin, but now they do not have to be a death sentence. As long as you are in the flesh of your sin-subjected body you will wrestle with sin, but sin no longer has to be your master. Instead, you can live with a higher purpose and the firm knowledge that you will have a joyful reunion with your Creator. Most importantly, as long as you are on earth, each day can bring growth in your relationship with your God. Because you were created for this relationship, you can be assured that nothing is more satisfying or more worth being your life's purpose.

Our Role: Section Summary

- *Our role in accepting the gift of salvation brokered by Christ is not a role of "doing" but a role of believing. We cannot accept the gift unless we believe in the person, the identity, and the personal application of Christ. This belief is called "faith".*

- *Accepting the gift of salvation requires humility. It is a return to truth. We must give up the lies of self-god-hood and allow God's will to be restored to ruling authority over our will.*

- *Believing results in a major transformation in a person's heart. Although we will not be perfect, a changed life and the ongoing work of the Holy Spirit are evidence that we have given our lives to Christ.*

- *True belief in Christ is a total renewing of your being. The one who gives his or her heart to Christ becomes an entirely new being by Christ, like a change in your spiritual DNA. There is no reverse process.*

- *God needs only that moment of truth, that simple yet complete yielding from us to count us under the death of Christ. Our response, change, and gratitude are life-long, but salvation occurs in a moment and lasts forever.*

- *To be set apart from corruption is to become holy. To be holy is to have your purpose aligned with God's purpose for you.*

- *Reconciliation with your Creator is reconciliation to the purposes for which you were created. Though you will wrestle with sin in this life, sin will no longer be your master.*

OUR HOPE IN GRACE

If we were to title the heart of this gift of salvation which God has offered to us, we might call it "grace". Grace is like mercy but more mysterious. Whereas mercy allows a wretch to be spared his plight, grace lifts that wretch out of sin and secures him an identity among the divine ones. Grace is an extension of the very spirit of God. It is because of His grace towards us that God engages with us and treats us with great, eternal value.[1] Grace is evident in God's going so far as to offer us salvation and a permanent position with Him.

To help us understand grace, let us consider a story:

Once there was a kind and good king who ruled a prosperous kingdom. The king was known for enforcing the kingdom's laws with wisdom and unwavering justice. For many years, that kingdom had suffered ongoing attacks from a neighboring kingdom. That neighboring kingdom was known for lavish parties and debauchery as much as it was known for corruption. One evening, the good king heard a commotion near his kitchen. Upon inquiring as to the source of the commotion, he was informed that a thief had broken into the kitchen and had been caught trying to steal the very food which was being prepared for the king's dinner. As stealing was strictly forbidden, it was simply unheard of that any thief would be bold enough to break into the king's pantry, much less pilfer the king's own dinner. It was also known that the king was generous with his food and would give to any person who was in need. The servants, who were loyal to their king, were outraged! Who would try and steal from the king who so generously cared for his subjects? The king ordered that the thief be brought immediately before the throne where the king made his official judgments in matters of justice.

The good king was astonished when the angry servants dragged in not a surly bandit but instead a dirty, defiant, little girl. It was plain from her style of dress that the little girl was a foreigner, native to the wicked neighboring kingdom. How had she managed to get inside the city walls, not to mention into the castle keep and the king's own kitchen? At first, the little girl would say nothing. Then, the king descended from his throne and took the little girl's hand. He led her to a nearby chair and kneeled in front of her as he gently asked her about herself. The little girl began to haltingly tell her story. She was an orphan and had been much oppressed in the wicked kingdom where she used to live. As she scrounged about the streets of the wicked kingdom, she had heard hushed rumors of the just king and his good kingdom. Figuring she had nothing to lose, she stowed away on a trader's wagon, left her native city, and snuck inside the city walls of the good kingdom. She was sure the good king, if he was as kind as she had been told, would help her. However, she had no idea how to see him and ask for his help. Indeed, when she first saw the majesty of the good king's castle and his richly clothed, healthy servants, she realized that she was really just a dirty, orphan, beggar who had no business with this king. She felt ashamed and became afraid. Then, as her hunger increased, she also grew angry. When she witnessed the good food going into the castle's kitchen and smelled the fragrance of the cooking, she decided that the king must be proud and mean to keep his food to himself. She dashed across the street, into the kitchen door, and managed to grab two rolls and a leg of roast chicken (breaking several dishes in the process) before being tackled by the head chef.

As they heard her story, the servants' indignation died down. They grew embarrassed at their rough treatment of the little orphan and began to consider how they might have handled the situation differently. If only this little girl had known better, she could have asked any of them how to get something to eat and they would have sent her to the right place. Now, she had committed a criminal offense, for which the fine was large. According to the king's laws, only the criminal or immediate family members could pay fines on behalf of a criminal. This little girl had no money and no family. Surely the king would not send her to jail, would he? Could he overlook the law and have mercy on her?

A king might have mercy on a poor orphan girl caught stealing from his pantry if he feeds her rather than punishing her. Each of us can appreciate that sort of mercy. We would probably want to see that mercy for the little orphan girl even if the mercy violated the "justice" required by the law of the land.

But what if instead of simply having mercy and feeding her, the king actually adopts the orphan as his own daughter? What if he accepts her into his family, pays her debts according to the law, and makes her a royal princess - an heir to his kingdom among his other children? In doing so, he goes beyond mercy and demonstrates amazing grace. Such grace not only fulfills the law but restores the once forlorn orphan to the significance and carefree happiness intended for little children. The orphan, who was once scorned, is now a legally legitimate and delightful daughter to the king!

On a divine and eternal scale, such is the grace our Creator has shown to us. Although He found us as wretches, outcasts from Eden, and sin-riddled abusers of the free will He gave us, our Creator has done no less than offer us a place as co-heirs with Christ.[2]

Is it possible to correctly respond to being offered such grace?[3] The wretched orphan girl was lifted out of her misery and made a true princess not because of some inherent quality she exclusively possessed, but rather because of an inherent heart of grace the king possessed. Having been made princess and anticipating a place of further honor in the kingdom, how should she then live? Should she hoard her good things and not let anybody know what the king did for her? Should she return to her old ways and steal from the king who is now her father? Should she lord her position over other servants in the kingdom? What would it say about her if she flaunted her royal robes in the streets and tormented the orphans who were formerly her peers? Should she withhold food from the hungry, scoff at the lowly, oppress the poor, and demand ever-higher taxes from the subjects in the kingdom? Worse yet, should she harbor bitterness towards the king who saved her? Should she neglect to acknowledge him and ignore him when he speaks to her? Of course not!

If we are, by God's grace demonstrated in the sacrifice of Christ, made heirs to the very kingdom of God, how should we then live the remainder of our lives on earth? Receiving grace changes us. Either it humbles, inspires, empowers, and equips us to extend similar grace to others, or it reveals us as even worse than we appeared before such grace was extended to us. With God's help, let us become delightful adopted children to our Heavenly Father rather than children of exasperation and grief!

We who choose to receive the grace being offered by God are not obligated to appear deserving of what God has given. We could never appear deserving of being treated as more perfect than we really are. Rather, we are obligated to leave off the behaviors which showed us to be so far from God in the first place. This change occurs as God's Holy Spirit begins to work in us and change us. We are to embrace our new lives as citizens in a divine kingdom in which we joyfully serve the King who is infinitely good, perfectly just, and who withholds no good thing from us.[4] Just as a father delights in his loving children, we can be a delight to our Heavenly Father. The Spirit of God instructs and enables those saved by Christ to live and act according to the grace that saved them. As long as we are living in this corrupted world, that Spirit will always be at war with our inherently sinful spirits. As permanent citizens saved into God's kingdom, we are not thrown out of the kingdom for our struggles with sin any more than we were adopted into the kingdom for our attempts at righteousness.[5] Nevertheless, it is right and comforting to demonstrate gratitude for our salvation both for our own sake and for the sake of those who have not yet found Christ. What could be greater than showing a fellow wretch where to find eternal life?[6]

There is another reason why we must allow the Spirit of God to help us live out our grace. We are on a stage in front of spectators we cannot fathom. The angels and the heavenly beings are engaged observers who not only wait with baited breath to see the outworking of God's marvelous plan, but who also rejoice when we humans appropriately glorify God.[7] What we do reflects God's work to an audience much larger than ourselves. With either excitement or horror, we can anticipate full revelation of our hearts on a universal stage. This universal revelation will occur when Jesus Christ returns as He has promised.[8]

As long as we are on this earth, our hope is in Christ. We not only place our hope in Him for our salvation, but we eagerly look forward to casting off our sinful flesh and being with Him forever.[9] When we consider He who made us and that He placed eternity in our hearts, we can be certain that an eternity with God, our Creator, our constant Pursuer, our Provider, our Savior, and our Heavenly Father, is an eternity worth any cost.

Our Hope in Grace: Section Summary

- *Grace is what removes us from a wretched state and lifts us to a new life with a divine identity. It goes beyond mercy and supersedes our human inclination of "justice".*

- *Once we have been saved, we spend the rest of our lives living in response to the staggering grace that saved us. We cannot earn or deserve our salvation, but if we continue embracing corruption then we appear to have missed the point.*

- *Our lives and behaviors are changed in an ongoing process by the work of God's Holy Spirit in our hearts. His Spirit will always be in conflict with the natural corruption we inherited in our sinful state. Though we will fail regularly, we must fight to keep the Holy Spirit in a position of authority and not give in to our contrary inclination to sin.*

- *We live in a larger context than we can imagine. Angels and heavenly beings are watching to see how we respond to our creator. We bring rightful glory to God by following Him as the one true God of the universe.*

CONCLUSION

I cannot possibly summarize a conclusion of these matters better than a certain other man who, long ago, also wrote to friends he had never met but already considered dear:

Therefore, there is now no condemnation for those who are in Christ Jesus, because through Christ Jesus the law of the Spirit who gives life has set you free from the law of sin and death. For what the law was powerless to do because it was weakened by the flesh, God did by sending His own Son in the likeness of sinful flesh to be a sin offering. And so He condemned sin in the flesh, in order that the righteous requirement of the law might be fully met in us, who do not live according to the flesh but according to the Spirit.

Those who live according to the flesh have their minds set on what the flesh desires; but those who live in accordance with the Spirit have their minds set on what the Spirit desires. The mind governed by the flesh is death, but the mind governed by the Spirit is life and peace. The mind governed by the flesh is hostile to God; it does not submit to God's law, nor can it do so. Those who are in the realm of the flesh cannot please God.

You, however, are not in the realm of the flesh but are in the realm of the Spirit, if indeed the Spirit of God lives in you. And if anyone does not have the Spirit of Christ, they do not belong to Christ. But if Christ is in you, then even though your body is subject to death because of sin, the Spirit gives life because of righteousness. And if the Spirit of Him who raised Jesus from the dead is living in you, He who raised Christ from the dead will also give life to your mortal bodies because of His Spirit who lives in you.

Therefore, brothers and sisters, we have an obligation – but it is not to the flesh, to live according to it. For if you live according to the flesh, you will die; but if by the Spirit you put to death the misdeeds of the body, you will live.

For those who are led by the Spirit of God are the children of God. The Spirit you received does not make you slaves, so that you live in fear again; rather, the Spirit you received brought about your adoption to sonship. And by Him we cry, "Abba, Father." The Spirit Himself testifies with our spirit that we are God's children. Now if we are children, then we are heirs – heirs of God and co-heirs with Christ, if indeed we share in His sufferings in order that we may also share in His glory.

I consider that our present sufferings are not worth comparing with the glory that will be revealed in us. For the creation waits in eager expectation for the children of God to be revealed. For the creation was subjected to frustration, not by its own choice, but by the will of the one who subjected it, in hope that the creation itself will be liberated from its bondage to decay and brought into the freedom and glory of the children of God.

We know that the whole creation has been groaning as in the pains of childbirth right up to the present time. Not only so, but we ourselves, who have the firstfruits of the Spirit, groan inwardly as we wait eagerly for our adoption to sonship, the redemption of our bodies. For in this hope we were saved. But hope that is seen is no hope at all. Who hopes for what they already have? But if we hope for what we do not yet have, we wait for it patiently.

In the same way, the Spirit helps us in our weakness. We do not know what we ought to pray for, but the Spirit Himself intercedes for us through wordless groans. And He who searches our hearts knows the mind of the Spirit, because the Spirit intercedes for God's people in accordance with the will of God.

And we know that in all things God works for the good of those who love Him, who have been called according to His purpose. For those God foreknew He also predestined to be conformed to the image of his Son, that He might be the firstborn among many brothers and sisters. And those He predestined, He also called; those He called, He also justified; those He justified, He also glorified.

What, then, shall we say in response to these things? If God is for us, who can be against us? He who did not spare His own Son, but gave Him up for us all – how will He not also, along with Him, graciously give us all things? Who will bring any charge against those whom God has chosen? It is God who justifies. Who then is the one who condemns? No one. Christ Jesus who died – more than that, who was raised to life – is at the right hand of God and is also interceding for us. Who shall separate us from the love of Christ? Shall trouble or hardship or persecution or famine or nakedness or danger or sword? As it is written:

> *"For your sake we face death all day long; we are considered as sheep to be slaughtered."*

No, in all these things we are more than conquerors through Him who loved us. For I am convinced that neither death nor life, neither angels nor demons, neither the present nor the future, nor any powers, neither height nor depth, nor anything else in all creation, will be able to separate us from the love of God that is in Christ Jesus our Lord.

(Quoted excerpt from Paul's letter to the Christians in Rome, A.D. 57. Romans chapter 8 as translated in the NIV)

APPENDIX

All scripture quotations are based on the NIV, which is copyrighted by Biblica, 2011.

Who is God?

1: You are worthy, our Lord and God, to receive glory and honor and power, for you created all things, and by your will they were created and have their being." (Revelation 4:11)

2: For you [God] created my inmost being; you knit me together in my mother's womb. I praise you because I am fearfully and wonderfully made; your works are wonderful, I know that full well. (Psalm 139:13-14)

3: But He [God] stands alone, and who can oppose him? He does whatever He pleases. (Job 23:13)

4: Who can fathom the Spirit of the LORD, or instruct the LORD as his counselor? Whom did the LORD consult to enlighten him, and who taught him the right way? Who was it that taught him knowledge, or showed him the path of understanding? (Isaiah 40:13-14)

5: Oh, the depth of the riches of the wisdom and knowledge of God! How unsearchable his judgments, and His paths beyond tracing out! (Romans 11:33)

6: God is not human, that He should lie, not a human being, that He should change his mind. Does He speak and then not act? Does he promise and not fulfill? (Numbers 23:19)

7: But the plans of the LORD stand firm forever, the purposes of His heart through all generations. (Psalm 33:11)

8: You are my witnesses," declares the LORD, "that I am God. "Yes, and from ancient days I am He. No one can deliver out of my hand. When I act, who can reverse it?" (Isaiah 43:12-13)

9: I, the LORD, speak the truth; I declare what is right. (Isaiah 45:19)

10: They will say of me, "In the LORD alone are deliverance and strength." All who have raged against Him will come to Him and be put to shame. (Isaiah 45:24)

11: You [God] are good, and what you do is good. (Psalm 119:68)

12: All your [God's] words are true; all your righteous laws are eternal. (Psalm 119:160)

13: "This is what the LORD says…"do you question me about my children, or give me orders about the work of my hands? It is I who made the earth and created mankind on it. My own hands stretched out the heavens; I marshaled their starry hosts." (Isaiah 45:11-12)

14: Your [God's] statutes are always righteous; give me understanding that I may live. (Psalm 119:144)

15: By myself I [God] have sworn, my mouth has uttered in all integrity a word that will not be revoked: Before me every knee will bow; by me every tongue will swear. (Isaiah 45:23)

16: Lift up your eyes to the heavens, look at the earth beneath; the heavens will vanish like smoke, the earth will wear out like a garment and its inhabitants die like flies. But my [God's] salvation will last forever, my righteousness will never fail. Hear me, you who know what is right, you people who have taken my instruction to heart: Do not fear the reproach of mere mortals or be terrified by their insults. For the moth will eat them up like a garment; the worm will devour them like wool. But my righteousness will last forever, my salvation through all generations. (Isaiah 45:6-8)

17: I [God], even I, am He who comforts you. Who are you that you fear mere mortals, human beings who are but grass, that you forget the LORD your Maker, who stretches out the heavens and who lays the foundations of the earth… (Isaiah 51:12-13)

18: This is what the LORD says… I am the first and I am the last; apart from me there is no God. (Isaiah 44:6)

19: "You are my witnesses," declares the LORD, "and my servant whom I have chosen, so that you may know and believe me and understand that I am He. Before me no god was formed, nor will there be one after me. (Isaiah 43:10)

20: Woe to those who quarrel with their Maker, those who are nothing but potsherds among the potsherds on the ground. Does the clay say to the potter, 'What are you making?' Does your work say, 'The potter has no hands'? (Isaiah 45:9)

21: Remember the former things, those of long ago; I am God, and there is no other; I am God, and there is none like me. I make known the end from the beginning, from ancient times, what is still to come. I say, 'My purpose will stand, and I will do all that I please.' (Isaiah 46:9-10)

22: But God was very angry when he [Balaam] went, and the angel of the LORD stood in the road to oppose him. (Numbers 22:22)

23: Do not worship any other god, for the LORD, whose name is Jealous, is a jealous God. (Exodus 34:14)

24: Have mercy on me, O God, according to your unfailing love; according to your great compassion blot out my transgressions. (Psalm 51:1)

25: Whoever does not love does not know God, because God is love. (1 John 4:8)

26: The LORD God said, "It is not good for the man to be alone. I will make a helper suitable for him." (Genesis 2:18)

27: Then God said, "Let us make mankind in our image, in our likeness…" (Genesis 1:26)

Our Relationship with God

1: Then the LORD God made a woman from the rib He had taken out of the man, and He brought her to the man. (Genesis 2:22)

2: The man said, "This is now bone of my bones and flesh of my flesh; she shall be called 'woman,' for she was taken out of man." (Genesis 2:23)

3: God blessed them and said to them, "Be fruitful and increase in number; fill the earth and subdue it. Rule over the fish in the sea and the birds in the sky and over every living creature that moves on the ground." (Genesis 1:28)

4: "As surely as I live, declares the Sovereign LORD, I take no pleasure in the death of the wicked, but rather that they turn from their ways and live. Turn! Turn from your evil ways!" (Ezekiel 33:11); "For I take no pleasure in the death of anyone, declares the Sovereign LORD. Repent and live!" (Ezekiel 18:32)

5: "Consider the ravens: They do not sow or reap, they have no storeroom or barn; yet God feeds them. And how much more valuable you are than birds!"(Luke 12:24); "...that we may live peaceful and quiet lives in all godliness and holiness. This is good, and pleases God our Savior, who wants all people to be saved and to come to a knowledge of the truth." (1 Timothy 2:2-4)

6: We love because He [God] first loved us. (1 John 4:19)

7: The LORD God made all kinds of trees grow out of the ground—trees that were pleasing to the eye and good for food. In the middle of the garden were the tree of life and the tree of the knowledge of good and evil. (Genesis 2:9)

8: The LORD God took the man and put him in the Garden of Eden to work it and take care of it. And the LORD God commanded the man, "You are free to eat from any tree in the garden; but you must not eat from the tree of the knowledge of good and evil, for when you eat from it you will certainly die." (Genesis 2:15-17)

9: Then the LORD God formed a man from the dust of the ground and breathed into his nostrils the breath of life, and the man became a living being. (Genesis 2:7)

Broken Relationship and the Oldest Lie in the Book

1: Do not be afraid of those who kill the body but cannot kill the soul. Rather, be afraid of the One who can destroy both soul and body in hell. (Matthew 10:28)

2: This is what the Sovereign LORD says to these bones: "I will make breath enter you, and you will come to life. I will attach tendons to you and make flesh come upon you and cover you with skin; I will put breath in you, and you will come to life. Then you will know that I am the LORD." (Ezekiel 37:5-6)

3: Your heart became proud on account of your beauty, and you corrupted your wisdom because of your splendor. So I [God] threw you to the earth; I made a spectacle of you before kings. (Ezekiel 28:17)

4: He seized the dragon, that ancient serpent, who is the devil, or Satan, and bound him for a thousand years. (Revelation 20:2)

5: You [Satan] were in Eden, the garden of God; every precious stone adorned you:...Your settings and mountings were made of gold; on the day you were created they were prepared. You were anointed as a guardian cherub, for so I [God] ordained you. You were on the holy mount of God; you walked among the fiery stones. You were blameless in your ways from the day you were created till wickedness was found in you...Your heart became proud on account of your beauty, and you corrupted your wisdom because of your splendor. So I threw you to the earth... (Ezekiel 28:13-15, 17)

6: "You boast, 'We have entered into a covenant with death, with the realm of the dead we have made an agreement. When an overwhelming scourge sweeps by, it cannot touch us, for we have made a lie our refuge and falsehood our hiding place.'" (Isaiah 28:15); "You said, 'I am forever— the eternal queen!' But you did not consider these things or reflect on what might happen." (Isaiah 47:7)

7: You have trusted in your wickedness and have said, 'No one sees me.' Your wisdom and knowledge mislead you when you say to yourself, 'I am, and there is none besides me.' (Isaiah 47:10)

8: Your covenant with death will be annulled; your agreement with the realm of the dead will not stand. When the overwhelming scourge sweeps by, you will be beaten down by it. (Isaiah 28:18)

9: In the pride of your heart you say, "I am a god; I sit on the throne of a god in the heart of the seas." But you are a mere mortal and not a god, though you think you are as wise as a god. (Ezekiel 28:1)

10: Turn to me and be saved, all you ends of the earth; for I am God, and there is no other. (Isaiah 45:22)

11: As for God, His way is perfect: The LORD's word is flawless. (2 Samuel 22:31; Psalm 18:30)

12: The arrogant cannot stand in your [God's] presence. (Psalm 5:5)

13: He [God] is the Rock, His works are perfect, and all His ways are just. A faithful God who does no wrong, upright and just is He. (Deuteronomy 32:4)

Separation from God

1: Do not conform to the pattern of this world, but be transformed by the renewing of your mind. Then you will be able to test and approve what God's will is—His good, pleasing and perfect will. (Romans 12:2)

2: The law of the LORD is perfect, refreshing the soul. The statutes of the LORD are trustworthy, making wise the simple. (Psalm 19:7)

Our Position on a Standard of Righteousness

1: Whoever keeps the whole law and yet stumbles at just one point is guilty of breaking all of it. (James 2:10)

2: All of us also lived among them at one time, gratifying the cravings of our flesh and following its desires and thoughts. Like the rest, we were by nature deserving of wrath. (Ephesians 2:3); So then, I myself in my mind am a slave to God's law, but in my sinful nature a slave to the law of sin. (Romans 7:25)

3: Surely I was sinful at birth, sinful from the time my mother conceived me. (Psalm 51:5)

4: Your [God's] eyes are too pure to look on evil; you cannot tolerate wrongdoing. (Habakkuk 1:13)

5: Can a mortal be more righteous than God? Can even a strong man be more pure than his Maker? (Job 4:17)

6: For I know my transgressions, and my sin is always before me. Against you [God], you only, have I sinned and done what is evil in your sight; so you are right in your verdict and justified when you judge. (Psalm 51:2-4); The [human] heart is deceitful above all things and beyond cure. Who can understand it? (Jeremiah 17:9); "For my thoughts are not your thoughts, neither are your ways my ways," declares the LORD. "As the heavens are higher than the earth, so are my ways higher than your ways and my thoughts than your thoughts." (Isaiah 55:8-9)

Forgiveness vs. Justice

1: The LORD loves righteousness and justice; the earth is full of his unfailing love. (Psalm 33:5); The heavens proclaim His [God's] righteousness, for He is a God of justice (Psalm 50:6); Righteousness and justice are the foundation of your [God's] throne; love and faithfulness go before you. (Psalm 89:14); I [God] will make justice the measuring line and righteousness the plumb line. (Isaiah 28:17)

2: And will not God bring about justice for His chosen ones, who cry out to Him day and night? Will He keep putting them off? (Luke 18:7)

3: Do not bring your [God's] servant into judgment, for no one living is righteous before you. (Psalm 143:2)

Protocol

1: I remember, LORD, your ancient laws, and I find comfort in them.; You reject all who stray from your decrees, for their delusions come to nothing. All the wicked of the earth you discard like dross; therefore I love your statutes. My flesh trembles in fear of you; I stand in awe of your laws. (Psalm 119:52; 118-120)

2: If perfection could have been attained through the Levitical priesthood—and indeed the law given to the people established that priesthood—why was there still need for another priest to come, one in the order of Melchizedek, not in the order of Aaron? (Hebrews 7:11)

3: Therefore no one will be declared righteous in God's sight by the works of the law; rather, through the law we become conscious of our sin. (Romans 3:20)

4: LORD, the God of Israel, you are righteous! We are left this day as a remnant. Here we are before you in our guilt, though because of it not one of us can stand in your presence. (Ezra 9:15)

5: I wait for your salvation, LORD, and I follow your commands. (Psalm 119:166)

6: For the life of a creature is in the blood, and I have given it to you to make atonement for yourselves on the altar; it is the blood that makes atonement for one's life. (Leviticus 17:11); For the wages of sin is death, but the gift of God is eternal life in Christ Jesus our Lord. (Romans 6:23)

7: Have mercy on me, O God, according to your unfailing love; according to your great compassion blot out my transgressions. (Psalm 51:1)

8: The former regulation is set aside because it was weak and useless (for the law made nothing perfect), and a better hope is introduced, by which we draw near to God. (Hebrews 7:18-19)

A World apart from its Creator

1: All have sinned and fall short of the glory of God. (Romans 3:23); We all, like sheep, have gone astray, each of us has turned to our own way; and the LORD has laid on Him the iniquity of us all. (Isaiah 53:6)

2: For I command you today to love the LORD your God, to walk in obedience to Him, and to keep His commands, decrees and laws; then you will live and increase, and the LORD your God will bless you in the land you are entering to possess. (Deuteronomy 30:16); One thing God has spoken, two things I have heard: "Power belongs to you, God, and with you, Lord, is unfailing love"; and, "You reward everyone according to what they have done. (Psalm 62:11-12)

3: Those of you who are left will waste away in the lands of their enemies because of their sins; also because of their ancestors' sins they will waste away. (Leviticus 26:39); For you write down bitter things against me and make me reap the sins of my youth…"So man wastes away like something rotten, like a garment eaten by moths. (Job 13:26-28)

4: Because of your [God's] wrath there is no health in my body; there is no soundness in my bones because of my sin. My guilt has overwhelmed me like a burden too heavy to bear. (Psalm 38:3-4)

5: The LORD saw how great the wickedness of the human race had become on the earth, and that every inclination of the thoughts of the human heart was only evil all the time. (Genesis 6:5)

6: For I am about to fall, and my pain is ever with me. I confess my iniquity; I am troubled by my sin. (Psalm 38:17-18)

7: Why is light given to those in misery, and life to the bitter of soul, to those who long for death that does not come, who search for it more than for hidden treasure, who are filled with gladness and rejoice when they reach the grave? (Job 3:20-22)

8: All of us have become like one who is unclean, and all our righteous acts are like filthy rags; we all shrivel up like a leaf, and like the wind our sins sweep us away. (Isaiah 64:6)

9: But now, Lord, what do I look for? My hope is in you. (Psalm 39:7)

10: How often they rebelled against Him in the wilderness and grieved Him in the wasteland! (Psalm 78:40)

11: For I [God] desire mercy, not sacrifice, and acknowledgment of God rather than burnt offerings. (Hosea 6:6)

12: The LORD does not look at the things people look at. People look at the outward appearance, but the LORD looks at the heart. (1 Samuel 16:7); Love the LORD your God with all your heart and with all your soul and with all your strength. (Deuteronomy 6:5)

13: You [God] open your hand and satisfy the desires of every living thing. The LORD is righteous in all His ways and faithful in all He does. The LORD is near to all who call on Him, to all who call on Him in truth. He fulfills the desires of those who fear Him; He hears their cry and saves them. (Psalm 145:16-19)

Hell and Heaven

1: Those who hate the LORD would cringe before Him, and their punishment would last forever. (Psalm 81:15); Do not be afraid of those who kill the body but cannot kill the soul. Rather, be afraid of the One who can destroy both soul and body in hell. (Matthew 10:28)

2: The wicked go down to the realm of the dead, all the nations that forget God. (Psalm 9:17)

3: You said in your heart, "I will ascend to the heavens; I will raise my throne above the stars of God; I will sit enthroned on the mount of assembly, on the utmost heights of Mount Zaphon. I will ascend above the tops of the clouds; I will make myself like the Most High." But you are brought down to the realm of the dead, to the depths of the pit. (Isaiah 14:13-15)

4: Consult God's instruction and the testimony of warning. If anyone does not speak according to this word, they have no light of dawn. Distressed and hungry, they will roam through the land; when they are famished, they will become enraged and, looking upward, will curse their king and their God. Then they will look toward the earth and see only distress and darkness and fearful gloom, and they will be thrust into utter darkness. (Isaiah 8:20-22)

5: Through your own fault you will lose the inheritance I [God] gave you. I will enslave you to your enemies in a land you do not know, for you have kindled my anger, and it will burn forever. (Jeremiah 17:4); Will you then say, "I am a god," in the presence of those who kill you? You will be but a mortal, not a god, in the hands of those who slay you. (Ezekiel 28:9); Are not my few days almost over? Turn away from me so I can have a moment's joy before I go to the place of no return, to the land of gloom and utter darkness, to the land of deepest night, of utter darkness and disorder, where even the light is like darkness. (Job 10:20-22)

6: Therefore Death expands its jaws, opening wide its mouth; into it will descend their nobles and masses with all their brawlers and revelers. (Isaiah 5:14)

7: If God places no trust in His servants, if He charges His angels with error, how much more those who live in houses of clay, whose foundations are in the dust, who are crushed more readily than a moth! Between dawn and dusk they are broken to pieces; unnoticed, they perish forever. (Job 4:18-20); Then Jesus began to denounce the towns in which most of His miracles had been performed, because they did not repent. "Woe to you, Chorazin! Woe to you, Bethsaida! For if the miracles that were performed in you had been performed in Tyre and Sidon, they would have repented long ago in sackcloth and ashes. But I tell you, it will be more bearable for Tyre and Sidon on the day of judgment than for you. And you, Capernaum, will you be lifted to the heavens? No, you will go down to Hades. For if the miracles that were performed in you had been performed in Sodom, it would have remained to this day. But I tell you that it will be more bearable for Sodom on the day of judgment than for you. (Matthew 11:20-24)

8: For I take no pleasure in the death of anyone, declares the Sovereign LORD. Repent and live! (Ezekiel 18:32); But unless you repent, you too will all perish. (Luke 13:5); LORD, do not your eyes look for truth? You struck them, but they felt no pain; you crushed them, but they refused correction. They made their faces harder than stone and refused to repent. (Jeremiah 5:3); But my [God's] people would not listen to me…So I gave them over to their stubborn hearts to follow their own devices. (Psalm 81:11-12)

9: "Well done, good and faithful servant! You have been faithful with a few things; I will put you in charge of many things. Come and share your master's happiness!" (Matthew 25:23); Jesus answered him, "Truly I tell you, today you will be with me in paradise." (Luke 23:43); We are confident, I say, and would prefer to be away from the body and at home with the Lord. (2 Corinthians 5:8); To the one who is victorious, I will give the right to eat from the tree of life, which is in the paradise of God. (Revelation 2:7); What no eye has seen, what no ear has heard, and what no human mind has conceived" — the things God has prepared for those who love him (1 Corinthians 2:9)

10: Do not hold against us the sins of past generations; may your mercy come quickly to meet us, for we are in desperate need. Help us, God our Savior, for the glory of your name; deliver us and forgive our sins for your name's sake. (Psalm 79:8-9)

Natural Consequences and the Devil's Role

1: For the wages of sin is death, but the gift of God is eternal life in Christ Jesus our Lord. (Romans 6:23); This was the sin of the house of Jeroboam that led to its downfall and to its destruction from the face of the earth. (1 Kings 13:34); If you do what is right, will you not be accepted? But if you do not do what is right, sin is crouching at your door; it desires to have you, but you must rule over it. (Genesis 4:7)

2: The great dragon was hurled down—that ancient serpent called the devil, or Satan, who leads the whole world astray. He was hurled to the earth, and his angels with him. (Revelation 12:9)

3: The one who does what is sinful is of the devil, because the devil has been sinning from the beginning. The reason the Son of God appeared was to destroy the devil's work. (1 John 3:8); Satan himself masquerades as an angel of light. (2 Corinthians 11:14); The field is the world, and the good seed stands for the people of the kingdom. The weeds are the people of the evil one, and the enemy who sows them is the devil. The harvest is the end of the age, and the harvesters are angels. (Matthew 13:38-39)

4: Then God said, "Let us make mankind in Our image, in Our likeness, so that they may rule over the fish in the sea and the birds in the sky, over the livestock and all the wild animals, and over all the creatures that move along the ground." So God created mankind in his own image, in the image of God He created them; male and female He created them. (Genesis 1:26-27)

5: You [those who will not hear what Jesus says] belong to your father, the devil, and you want to carry out your father's desires. He was a murderer from the beginning, not holding to the truth, for there is no truth in him. When he lies, he speaks his native language, for he is a liar and the father of lies. (John 8:44); They had as king over them the angel of the Abyss, whose name in Hebrew is Abaddon and in Greek is Apollyon (that is, Destroyer). (Revelation 9:11); Be alert and of sober mind. Your enemy the devil prowls around like a roaring lion looking for someone to devour. (1 Peter 5:8); Simon, Simon, Satan has asked to sift all of you as wheat. (Luke 22:31)

6: No temptation has overtaken you except what is common to mankind. (1 Corinthians 10:13); The god of this age [Satan] has blinded the minds of unbelievers, so that they cannot see the light of the gospel that displays the glory of Christ, who is the image of God. (2 Corinthians 4:4)

7: The LORD looks down from heaven on all mankind to see if there are any who understand, any who seek God. All have turned away, all have become corrupt; there is no one who does good, not even one. (Psalm 14:2-3)

8: At midday you will grope about like a blind person in the dark. You will be unsuccessful in everything you do; day after day you will be oppressed and robbed, with no one to rescue you. (Deuteronomy 28:29)

9: I know that the LORD secures justice for the poor and upholds the cause of the needy. (Psalm 140:12); And I saw the dead, great and small, standing before the throne, and books were opened. Another book was opened, which is the book of life. The dead were judged according to what they had done as recorded in the books. (Revelation 20:12)

Debt versus Punishment

1: God does all these things to a person — twice, even three times — to turn them back from the pit, that the light of life may shine on them. (Job 33:29-30); And have you completely forgotten this word of encouragement that addresses you as a father addresses his son? It says, "My son, do not make light of the Lord's discipline, and do not lose heart when He rebukes you, because the Lord disciplines the one He loves, and He chastens everyone He accepts as His son. (Hebrews 12:5-6)

The Cost of Reconciliation

1: Though they offer sacrifices as gifts to Me, and though they eat the meat, the LORD is not pleased with them. Now He will remember their wickedness and punish their sins. (Hosea 8:13); When you offer blind animals for sacrifice, is that not wrong? When you sacrifice lame or diseased animals, is that not wrong? Try offering them to your governor! Would he be pleased with you? Would he accept you?" says the LORD Almighty. Now plead with God to be gracious to us. With such offerings from your hands, will He accept you?"—says the LORD Almighty. "Oh, that one of you would shut the temple doors, so that you would not light useless fires on my altar! I am not pleased with you," says the LORD Almighty, "and I will accept no offering from your hands… "When you bring injured, lame or diseased animals and offer them as sacrifices, should I accept them from your hands?" says the LORD (Malachi 1:8-10, 13)

2: [Christ Jesus] Who, being in very nature God, did not consider equality with God something to be used to His own advantage; rather, He made Himself nothing by taking the very nature of a servant, being made in human likeness. And being found in appearance as a man, He humbled Himself by becoming obedient to death— even death on a cross! (Philippians 2:6-7)

3: Where were you when I laid the earth's foundation? Tell me, if you understand. Who marked off its dimensions? Surely you know! Who stretched a measuring line across it? On what were its footings set, or who laid its cornerstone— while the morning stars sang together and all the angels shouted for joy. (Job 38:6-7); You alone are the LORD. You made the heavens, even the highest heavens, and all their starry host, the earth and all that is on it, the seas and all that is in them. You give life to everything, and the multitudes of heaven worship you. (Nehemiah 9:6)

4: He has made everything beautiful in its time. He has also set eternity in the human heart; yet no one can fathom what God has done from beginning to end. (Ecclesiastes 3:11)

5: This day I [God] call the heavens and the earth as witnesses against you that I have set before you life and death, blessings and curses. Now choose life, so that you and your children may live. (Deuteronomy 30:19); But if serving the LORD seems undesirable to you, then choose for yourselves this day whom you will serve, whether the gods your ancestors served beyond the Euphrates, or the gods of the Amorites, in whose land you are living. But as for me and my household, we will serve the LORD. (Joshua 24:15)

6: We saw the Nephilim there (the descendants of Anak come from the Nephilim). We seemed like grasshoppers in our own eyes, and we looked the same to them. (Numbers 13:33); A voice says, "Cry out." And I said, "What shall I cry?" "All people are like grass, and all their faithfulness is like the flowers of the field. The grass withers and the flowers fall, because the breath of the LORD blows on them. Surely the people are grass." (Isaiah 40:6-7)

7: Then the LORD said, "My Spirit will not contend with humans forever, for they are mortal; their days will be a hundred and twenty years." (Genesis 6:3); For all have sinned and fall short of the glory of God (Romans 3:23)

8: His [God's] intent was that now, through the church, the manifold wisdom of God should be made known to the rulers and authorities in the heavenly realms… (Ephesians 3:10)

Terms of Redemption

1: There is no difference between Jew and Gentile, for all have sinned and fall short of the glory of God, and all are justified freely by His grace through the redemption that came by Christ Jesus. God presented Christ as a sacrifice of atonement, through the shedding of his blood—to be received by faith. He did this to demonstrate His righteousness, because in His forbearance He had left the sins committed beforehand unpunished— He did it to demonstrate His righteousness at the present time, so as to be just and the one who justifies those who have faith in Jesus. (Romans 3:22-26)

2: Do we, then, nullify the law by this faith? Not at all! Rather, we uphold the law. (Romans 3:31)

3: Yet it was the LORD's will to crush Him and cause Him to suffer, and though the LORD makes His life an offering for sin, He will see his offspring and prolong His days, and the will of the LORD will prosper in His hand. (Isaiah 53:10)

4: The reason my Father loves me [Jesus] is that I lay down my life—only to take it up again. No one takes it from me, but I lay it down of my own accord. I have authority to lay it down and authority to take it up again.

This command I received from my Father." (John 10:17)

5: For He [Christ Jesus] Himself is our peace, who has made the two groups [Jews and Gentiles] one and has destroyed the barrier, the dividing wall of hostility, by setting aside in His flesh the law with its commands and regulations. His purpose was to create in Himself one new humanity out of the two, thus making peace, and in one body to reconcile both of them to God through the cross, by which He put to death their hostility. He came and preached peace to you who were far away and peace to those who were near. For through Him we both have access to the Father by one Spirit. (Ephesians 2:14-18)

Jesus Christ

1: The Son is the image of the invisible God, the firstborn over all creation. For in Him all things were created: things in heaven and on earth, visible and invisible, whether thrones or powers or rulers or authorities; all things have been created through Him and for Him. He is before all things, and in Him all things hold together. (Colossians 1:15-17)

2: And being found in appearance as a man, He [Christ Jesus] humbled Himself by becoming obedient to death— even death on a cross! (Philippians 2:8)

3: For God was pleased to have all His fullness dwell in Him [Jesus Christ], and through Him to reconcile to Himself all things, whether things on earth or things in heaven, by making peace through His blood, shed on the cross. (Colossians 1:19-20)

4: God made Him who had no sin to be sin for us, so that in Him we might become the righteousness of God. (2 Corinthians 5:21); So Jesus said, "When you have lifted up the Son of Man, then you will know that I am He and that I do nothing on my own but speak just what the Father has taught me. (John 8:28); For we do not have a high priest who is unable to empathize with our weaknesses, but we have one who has been tempted in every way, just as we are—yet He did not sin. (Hebrews 4:15)

5: When He [Jesus] had finished washing their [His disciples'] feet, He put on His clothes and returned to His place. "Do you understand what I have done for you?" He asked them. "You call me 'Teacher' and 'Lord,' and rightly so, for that is what I am. Now that I, your Lord and Teacher, have washed your feet, you also should wash one another's feet. I have set you an example that you should do as I have done for you." (John 13:12-15)

6: He [the Messiah, or Christ] had no beauty or majesty to attract us to Him, nothing in His appearance that we should desire Him. He was despised and rejected by mankind, a man of suffering, and familiar with pain. Like one from whom people hide their faces He was despised, and we held Him in low esteem. (Isaiah 53:2-3)

7: So He [Jesus] replied to the messengers, "Go back and report to John what you have seen and heard: The blind receive sight, the lame walk, those who have leprosy are cleansed, the deaf hear, the dead are raised, and the good news is proclaimed to the poor. (Luke 7:22); Jesus said to them, "I have shown you many good works from the Father. For which of these do you stone me?" (John 10:32)

8: Then Jesus declared, "I am the bread of life. Whoever comes to me will never go hungry, and whoever believes in me will never be thirsty." (John 6:35); But He [Jesus] continued, "You are from below; I am from above. You are of this world; I am not of this world. I told you that you would die in your sins; if you do not believe that I am He, you will indeed die in your sins." (John 8:23-24); Very truly I [Jesus] tell you, whoever obeys my word will never see death. (John 8:51); My Father, whom you claim as your God, is the one who glorifies me [Jesus]. Though you do not know Him, I know him. If I said I did not, I would be a liar like you, but I do know Him and obey His word. Your father Abraham rejoiced at the thought of seeing my day; he saw it and was glad." "You are not yet fifty years old," they said to him, "and you have seen Abraham!" "Very truly I tell you, "Jesus answered, "before Abraham was born, I am!" At this, they picked up stones to stone him, but Jesus hid Himself, slipping away from the temple grounds. (John 8:54-59)

9: Jesus, knowing that they intended to come and make Him king by force, withdrew again to a mountain by Himself. (John 6:15); I am the gate; whoever enters through me will be saved. They will come in and go out, and find pasture. The thief comes only to steal and kill and destroy; I have come that they may have life, and have it to the full. (John 10:9-10)

10: In that hour Jesus said to the crowd, "Am I leading a rebellion, that you have come out with swords and clubs to capture me? Every day I sat in the temple courts teaching, and you did not arrest me. But this has all taken place that the writings of the prophets might be fulfilled." Then all the disciples deserted Him and fled. (Matthew 26:55-56)

11: Then the Pharisees went out and began to plot with the Herodians how they might kill Jesus. (Mark 3:6)

12: "What shall I do, then, with Jesus who is called the Messiah?" Pilate asked. They all answered, "Crucify Him!" "Why? What crime has He committed?" asked Pilate. But they shouted all the louder, "Crucify Him!" (Matthew 27:22-23)

13: "Do not suppose that I [Jesus] have come to bring peace to the earth. I did not come to bring peace, but a sword. For I have come to turn" 'a man against his father, a daughter against her mother, a daughter-in-law against her mother-in-law— a man's enemies will be the members of his own household.' "Anyone who loves their father or mother more than me is not worthy of me; anyone who loves their son or daughter more than me is not worthy of me. Whoever does not take up their cross and follow me is not worthy of me. Whoever finds their life will lose it, and whoever loses their life for my sake will find it. (Matthew 10:34-39)

14: He [Jesus] is not here; He has risen! Remember how He told you [disciples], while He was still with you in Galilee: 'The Son of Man must be delivered over to the hands of sinners, be crucified and on the third day be raised again.' "Then they remembered His words. (Luke 24:6-8)

15: He was oppressed and afflicted, yet He did not open His mouth; He was led like a lamb to the slaughter, and as a sheep before its shearers is silent, so He did not open His mouth. By oppression and judgment He was taken away. Yet who of His generation protested? For He was cut off from the land of the living; for the transgression of my people He was punished. (Isaiah 53:7-9)

16: For Christ also suffered once for sins, the righteous for the unrighteous, to bring you to God. He was put to death in the body but made alive in the Spirit. (1 Peter 3:18); The death He died, He died to sin once for all; but the life He lives, He lives to God. (Romans 6:10)

17: Jesus answered, "I am the way and the truth and the life. No one comes to the Father except through me." (John 14:6)

18: "I [Jesus] have not come to call the righteous, but sinners to repentance." (Luke 5:32)

19: Jesus said to her, "I am the resurrection and the life. The one who believes in me will live, even though they die; and whoever lives by believing in me will never die. Do you believe this?" (John 11:25-26)

20: We [who are alive in Christ] are those who have died to sin; how can we live in it any longer? (Romans 6:2); This is why "it was credited to him [Abraham] as righteousness." The words "it was credited to him" were written not for him alone, but also for us, to whom God will credit righteousness—for us who believe in Him who raised Jesus our Lord from the dead. (Romans 4:22-24)

21: God made Him who had no sin to be sin for us, so that in Him we might become the righteousness of God. (2 Corinthians 5:21)

22: It is for freedom that Christ has set us free. Stand firm, then, and do not let yourselves be burdened again by a yoke of slavery. (Galations 5:1)

23: Christ redeemed us from the curse of the law by becoming a curse for us…(Galatians 3:13); I do not set aside the grace of God, for if righteousness could be gained through the law, Christ died for nothing! (Galatians 2:21)

24: Christ is the culmination of the law so that there may be righteousness for everyone who believes. (Romans 10:4)

25: …and giving joyful thanks to the Father, who has qualified you to share in the inheritance of His holy people in the kingdom of light. For He has rescued us from the dominion of darkness and brought us into the kingdom of the Son He loves, in whom we have redemption, the forgiveness of sins. (Colossians 1:12-13)

26: Whoever believes in Him is not condemned, but whoever does not believe stands condemned already because they have not believed in the name of God's one and only Son. (John 3:18)

27: ...according to His eternal purpose that He accomplished in Christ Jesus our Lord. In Him and through faith in Him we may approach God with freedom and confidence. (Ephesians 3:11-12)

28: For there is one God and one mediator between God and mankind, the man Christ Jesus, who gave Himself as a ransom for all people. (1 Timothy 2:5-6); Salvation is found in no one else, for there is no other name under heaven given to mankind by which we must be saved." (Acts 4:12)

A Caution

1: Beyond all question, the mystery from which true godliness springs is great: He appeared in the flesh, was vindicated by the Spirit, was seen by angels, was preached among the nations, was believed on in the world, was taken up in glory. (1 Timothy 3:16)

2: Jesus answered, "I am the way and the truth and the life. No one comes to the Father except through me. (John 14:6); I [Jesus] am the resurrection and the life. The one who believes in me will live, even though they die;

and whoever lives by believing in me will never die. Do you believe this? .(John 11:25-26)

3: My goal is that they may be encouraged in heart and united in love, so that they may have the full riches of complete understanding, in order that they may know the mystery of God, namely, Christ, in whom are hidden all the treasures of wisdom and knowledge. (Colossians 2:2-3)

4: If you declare with your mouth, "Jesus is Lord," and believe in your heart that God raised him from the dead, you will be saved. (Romans 10:9)

5: If I have the gift of prophecy and can fathom all mysteries and all knowledge, and if I have a faith that can move mountains, but do not have love, I am nothing. (1 Corinthians 13:12)

6: …you were bought at a price. (1 Corinthians 6:20)

7: Who can fathom the Spirit of the LORD, or instruct the LORD as His counselor? (Isaiah 40:13)

Proof

1: He will swallow up death forever. The Sovereign LORD will wipe away the tears from all faces; He will remove His people's disgrace from all the earth. The LORD has spoken. (Isaiah 25:8); who through the Spirit of holiness was appointed the Son of God in power by His resurrection from the dead: Jesus Christ our Lord. (Romans 1:4); For we believe that Jesus died and rose again, and so we believe that God will bring with Jesus those who have fallen asleep in Him. (1 Thessalonians 4:14) …just as Christ was raised from the dead through the glory of the Father, we too may live a new life. (Romans 6:4)

2: The soldiers therefore came and broke the legs of the first man who had been crucified with Jesus, and then those of the other. But when they came to Jesus and found that He was already dead, they did not break His legs. Instead, one of the soldiers pierced Jesus' side with a spear, bringing a sudden flow of blood and water. (John 19:32-34); Joseph of Arimathea, a prominent member of the Council, who was himself waiting for the kingdom of God, went boldly to Pilate and asked for Jesus' body. Pilate was surprised to hear that He was already dead. Summoning the centurion, he asked him if Jesus had already died. When he learned from the centurion that it was so, he gave the body to Joseph. (Mark 15:43-45)

3: …if Christ has not been raised, our preaching is useless and so is your faith. More than that, we are then found to be false witnesses about God, for we have testified about God that He raised Christ from the dead. But He did not raise him if in fact the dead are not raised. For if the dead are not raised, then Christ has not been raised either. And if Christ has not been raised, your faith is futile; you are still in your sins. Then those also who have fallen asleep in Christ are lost. If only for this life we have hope in Christ, we are of all people most to be pitied. But Christ has indeed been raised from the dead, the firstfruits of those who have fallen asleep. For since death came through a man, the resurrection of the dead comes also through a man. For as in Adam all die, so in Christ all will be made alive. But each in turn: Christ, the firstfruits; then, when He comes, those who belong to Him. (1 Corinthians 15:14-23)

4: He was delivered over to death for our sins and was raised to life for our justification. (Romans 4:25) For what I received I passed on to you as of first importance: that Christ died for our sins according to the Scriptures, that He was buried, that He was raised on the third day according to the Scriptures…(1 Corinthians 15:3-4)

5: …and…[after He was raised on the 3rd day] He [Jesus] appeared to Cephas, and then to the Twelve. After that, He appeared to more than five hundred of the brothers and sisters at the same time, most of whom are still living, though some have fallen asleep. Then He appeared to James, then to all the apostles, and last of all He appeared to me [Paul] also…(1 Corinthians 15:4-7); After His suffering, He (Jesus] presented Himself to them and gave many convincing proofs that He was alive. He appeared to them over a period of forty days and spoke about the kingdom of God. (Acts 1:3)

6: While the women were on their way, some of the guards went into the city and reported to the chief priests everything that had happened [Jesus' dramatic exit from the tomb]. When the chief priests had met with the elders and devised a plan, they gave the soldiers a large sum of money, telling them, "You are to say, 'His disciples came during the night and stole Him away while we were asleep.' If this report gets to the governor, we will satisfy him and keep you out of trouble." So the soldiers took the money and did as they were instructed. And this story has been widely circulated among the Jews to this very day. (Matthew 28:11-13)

7: "Take a guard," Pilate answered. "Go, make the tomb as secure as you know how." So they went and made the tomb secure by putting a seal on the stone and posting the guard. (Matthew 27:65-66)

8: There were others who were tortured, refusing to be released so that they might gain an even better resurrection. Some faced jeers and flogging, and even chains and imprisonment. They were put to death by stoning; they were sawed in two; they were killed by the sword. They went about in sheepskins and goatskins, destitute, persecuted and mistreated— the world was not worthy of them. They wandered in deserts and mountains, living in caves and in holes in the ground. (Hebrews 11:35-38)

Holy Spirit

1: When the day of Pentecost came, they [the 12 apostles] were all together in one place. Suddenly a sound like the blowing of a violent wind came from heaven and filled the whole house where they were sitting. They saw what seemed to be tongues of fire that separated and came to rest on each of them. All of them were filled with the Holy Spirit and began to speak in other tongues as the Spirit enabled them. (Acts 2:1-4)

2: We are witnesses of these things, and so is the Holy Spirit, whom God has given to those who obey Him. (Acts 5:32)

3: ...God anointed Jesus of Nazareth with the Holy Spirit and power, and how He went around doing good and healing all who were under the power of the devil, because God was with Him. (Acts 10:38)

4: God, who knows the heart, showed that He accepted them by giving the Holy Spirit to them, just as He did to us. (Acts 15:8); And we all, who with unveiled faces contemplate the Lord's glory, are being transformed into His image with ever-increasing glory, which comes from the Lord, who is the Spirit. (2 Corinthians 3:18)

5: …the Holy Spirit will teach you at that time what you should say. (Luke 12:12); But the Advocate, the Holy Spirit, whom the Father will send in my name, will teach you all things and will remind you of everything I have said to you. (John 14:26); At that time Jesus, full of joy through the Holy Spirit, said, "I praise you, Father, Lord of heaven and earth, because you have hidden these things from the wise and learned, and revealed them to little children. Yes, Father, for this is what you were pleased to do. (Luke 10:21); But you [disciples] will receive power when the Holy Spirit comes on you… (Acts 1:8)

6: And that is what some of you were. But you were washed, you were sanctified, you were justified in the name of the Lord Jesus Christ and by the Spirit of our God. (1 Corinthians 6:11)

7: And hope does not put us to shame, because God's love has been poured out into our hearts through the Holy Spirit, who has been given to us. (Romans 5:5)

8: And you also were included in Christ when you heard the message of truth, the gospel of your salvation. When you believed, you were marked in him with a seal, the promised Holy Spirit, who is a deposit guaranteeing our inheritance until the redemption of those who are God's possession—to the praise of His glory. (Ephesians 1:13-14)

9: And they [disciples] were all filled with the Holy Spirit and spoke the word of God boldly. (Acts 4:31)

10: For the grace of God has appeared that offers salvation to all people. (Titus 2:11); This righteousness is given through faith in Jesus Christ to all who believe. There is no difference between Jew and Gentile, for all have sinned and fall short of the glory of God, and all are justified freely by His grace through the redemption that came by Christ Jesus. God presented Christ as a sacrifice of atonement, through the shedding of His blood—to be received by faith. He did this to demonstrate His righteousness, because in His forbearance He had left the sins committed beforehand unpunished—He did it to demonstrate His righteousness at the present time, so as to be just and the one who justifies those who have faith in Jesus. (Romans 3:22-26)

11: For He says, "In the time of my favor I heard you, and in the day of salvation I helped you." I tell you, now is the time of God's favor, now is the day of salvation. (2 Corinthians 6:2)

Our Role

1: For God so loved the world that He gave His one and only Son, that whoever believes in Him shall not perish but have eternal life. (John 3:16)

2: "I will scatter you like chaff driven by the desert wind. This is your lot, the portion I have decreed for you," declares the LORD, "because you have forgotten me and trusted in false gods." (Jeremiah 13:24-25)

3: But God demonstrates His own love for us in this: While we were still sinners, Christ died for us. (Romans 5:8)

4: We love because He first loved us. (1 John 4:19)

5: For in the gospel the righteousness of God is revealed—a righteousness that is by faith from first to last, just as it is written: "The righteous will live by faith." (Romans 1:17)

6: ··according to His eternal purpose that He accomplished in Christ Jesus our Lord. In Him and through faith in Him we may approach God with freedom and confidence. (Ephesians 3:11-12)

7: In the same way, faith by itself, if it is not accompanied by action, is dead. (James 2:17)

8: Do you not know that your bodies are temples of the Holy Spirit, who is in you, whom you have received from God? You are not your own; you were bought at a price. Therefore honor God with your bodies. (1 Corinthians 6:19-20)

9: And that is what some of you were. But you were washed, you were sanctified, you were justified in the name of the Lord Jesus Christ and by the Spirit of our God. (1 Corinthians 6:11)

10: My [Jesus] sheep listen to my voice; I know them, and they follow me. I give them eternal life, and they shall never perish; no one will snatch them out of my hand. My Father, who has given them to me, is greater than all; no one can snatch them out of my Father's hand. I and the Father are one." (John 10:27-30)

11: Therefore, if anyone is in Christ, the new creation has come: The old has gone, the new is here! (2 Corinthians 5:17)

Our Hope in Grace

1: But because of His great love for us, God, who is rich in mercy, made us alive with Christ even when we were dead in transgressions—it is by grace you have been saved. (Ephesians 2:4-5)

2: The Spirit himself testifies with our spirit that we are God's children. Now if we are children, then we are heirs—heirs of God and co-heirs with Christ, if indeed we share in His sufferings in order that we may also share in His glory. (Romans 8: 16-17)

3: In Him we have redemption through His blood, the forgiveness of sins, in accordance with the riches of God's grace that He lavished on us. With all wisdom and understanding, He made known to us the mystery of His will according to His good pleasure, which He purposed in Christ, to be put into effect when the times reach their fulfillment—to bring unity to all things in heaven and on earth under Christ. (Ephesians 1:7-10)

4: See what great love the Father has lavished on us, that we should be called children of God! And that is what we are! The reason the world does not know us is that it did not know Him. (1 John 3:1); The lions may grow weak and hungry, but those who seek the LORD lack no good thing. (Psalm 34:10)

5: For it is by grace you have been saved, through faith—and this is not from yourselves, it is the gift of God—not by works, so that no one can boast. (Ephesians 2:8-9)

6: When you were slaves to sin, you were free from the control of righteousness. What benefit did you reap at that time from the things you are now ashamed of? Those things result in death! But now that you have been set free from sin and have become slaves of God, the benefit you reap leads to holiness, and the result is eternal life. (Romans 6:20-22)

7: In the same way, I [Jesus] tell you, there is rejoicing in the presence of the angels of God over one sinner who repents. (Luke 15:10); And God raised us up with Christ and seated us with Him in the heavenly realms in Christ Jesus, in order that in the coming ages He might show the incomparable riches of His grace, expressed in His kindness to us in Christ Jesus. (Ephesians 2:6-7)

8: They were looking intently up into the sky as He was going, when suddenly two men dressed in white stood beside them. "Men of Galilee," they said, "why do you stand here looking into the sky? This same Jesus, who has been taken from you into heaven, will come back in the same way you have seen Him go into heaven." (Acts 1:10-11); What good will it be for someone to gain the whole world, yet forfeit their soul? Or what can anyone give in exchange for their soul? For the Son of Man is going to come in His Father's glory with His angels, and then He will reward each person according to what they have done. (Matthew 16:26-27); …"'the sun will be darkened, and the moon will not give its light; the stars will fall from the sky, and the heavenly bodies will be shaken.' "At that time people will see the Son of Man coming in clouds with great power and glory. And He will send His angels and gather His elect from the four winds, from the ends of the earth to the ends of the heavens." (Mark 13:24-27)

9: One thing I ask from the LORD, this only do I seek: that I may dwell in the house of the LORD all the days of my life, to gaze on the beauty of the LORD and to seek Him in His temple. (Psalm 27:4)

Made in the USA
Charleston, SC
28 October 2013